SPIRIT

Intention & Path

As Seen through Martial Arts

by

Barry B Barker M.A., L.Ac.

Crystal Pointe Media Inc., San Diego, CA

Spirit: Intention & Path As Seen through Martial Arts

Barry B Barker, M.A., L.Ac.

Copyright © 2015

Originally Published in 2015: 2018 Updated Edition

Published by Crystal Pointe Media Inc.
San Diego, California

ISBN-13: 978-1541000018
ISBN-10: 1541000013

DISCLAIMER
The contents of this publication are intended to be educational and informative. They are not to be considered a directive to use Martial Arts on other individuals. Before embarking on Martial Arts training you should have clearance from your personal physician or health care provider then research and find competent instruction and training.

WARNING
This book and others in this series cover mature themes regarding Martial Art techniques, targets and methods that can do serious and irrevocable harm to another human being. Its use is only made available for Self-Defense and Sport Fighting purposes and should never be misapplied.

Cover Design by Daniel Barnier

ACKNOWLEDGEMENTS

Thank you GM Parker Linekin for your review of my books and for writing the Foreword that I chose to place in this book on the Spirit, Intention and Path.

My appreciation also goes out to my Black Belt student Dr. John Hippen, and Acupuncture colleague and friend, Brent Keime L.Ac., for reviewing and verifying parts of what I have written here. Thanks to my proofreaders for this book, Black Belt student Patty Alvarez, and Jennifer Nila.

In addition, I'm always thankful for my Black Belt sons Josh and Jordan for demonstrating their expertise in many of the video clips referenced throughout this book series. Love you guys.

Barry Barker, M.A., L.Ac.

DEDICATION

Friends & Memorable Times

Along with family, teachers, and students, it takes friends, classmates, their families, and acquaintances over many years of living, working, and training to lead a life dedicated to one's passion. It's easy and normal to stray from one's path at times but people come in and out of our lives, and events occur that keep us, or get us back to that journey.

There is a dynamic that makes for an always present bond even if some people are just seen occasionally, years later, or never again. These are the people who become an unexpected and invaluable part of our life's fabric.

They bring an energy and spirit that affects those around them, making them a part of someone else's life memories. This book is dedicated to those countless people throughout my life who have made it interesting, educational, fun, joyful, and sometimes painful. They are appreciated and never forgotten. Only some of my many pictures and memories are shown here and I only wish I could show more.

PREFACE

This is one of a three book series I gave myself as an advanced Black Belt thesis project, and for the personal growth I expected would accompany the effort. Another big project of mine was attaining a Master's Degree in Chinese Medicine and subsequent Acupuncture Licensing. Rank integrity is important so I am compelled to make a large effort towards that end. This I hope sets a good example for my children and my students.

My books are intended as a reference resource for my students, along with style related information for American Kenpo practitioners and Martial Arts enthusiasts in general as several chapters are on non-style related subjects (e.g. Concepts & Principles, Pressure Points, Sport Fighting, Martial Arts First Aid). Any athlete can also benefit from some of what is contained (e.g. Breathing, Balance, Exercise & Nutrition), or even curious observers may find something of interest (e.g. Qi, Yin/Yang).

This 3-book series is formatted using one of the oldest and most accepted martial art concepts with 3 components traditionally sought for development, the *Mind, Body,* and *Spirit.* This is the book of the *Spirit.*

My personal biography is at the back but my formal training began in 1973, but more consistently in 1980. I opened my Kenpo Karate School in 1984 (my full-time job for over 30 years as of this writing) and added a Sport Fighting Gym in 1998. These experiences have given me the background to write on the subjects covered in this and my other books.

During this time I have been able to put my entire system on video, so throughout my books there are (often colorful) names in parenthesis of techniques from my Kenpo system where whatever is being explained can be seen. Those videos are accessible at BarryBBarker.com.

I find martial arts, the culture, and the community that develops through it a fascinating subject that is not and never will be technology-based. This makes the information and knowledge timeless for each generation to learn during their own lifetime. My hope is that I can contribute to the martial art nexus for present and future generations so they can begin with a higher baseline of available accessible information.

The accumulation of knowledge, experience, and wisdom attained in this life continuum we all travel on, when infused with a dedicated spirit over a lifetime, can bring about the ultimate expertise in any field of endeavor. People who dedicate themselves in this way receive my highest admiration as I strive to be a worthy participant in my field.

FOREWORD
By Grand Master Parker Linekin

I have read Ed Parker's Infinite Insights book series and felt his work was amazing at describing principles and theories of Kenpo Karate. Barry Barker's book series take's descriptions of Kenpo theory, martial arts philosophy, and how to instruct to the next level.

He includes the mental, physical, and spiritual aspects of martial arts training, describing even neural point striking, something not often known or taught. I see this as a book for not only Kenpo students and instructors, but for all martial arts students who would like to study this vast subject in greater depth.

Ed Parker had a saying "he who dares to teach should never cease to learn." Barry epitomizes that saying. Brian Adam's, my instructor said, "respect all arts," Barry has done that as well. In my over 40 years of knowing Barry he has always had an open mind and is always learning. He is a Licensed Acupuncturist, has trained and taught Tai Chi, and continues to learn and refine his art. This is a great read for martial artists and non-martial artists alike. I highly recommend this book series.

Grandmaster Parker Linekin
10th Dan (Degree) Kenpo Karate
10th Dan White Tiger Tai Chi Chuan
5th Dan Daito Ryu Aiki Ju Jitsu
4th Dan Ching Yi Internal Boxing System
4th Dan Phan Ku Ju Jitsu, Southern Calif. Rep for Phan-ku

SPIRIT
TABLE OF CONTENTS

THE SPIRIT
Chapter 1

Spirit or Soul   **Competitive Spirit**

The idea or concept of Mind-Body-Spirit as an integrated whole is a common thread that transcends most martial arts styles and practitioners. It is used and referenced on a regular basis in the teaching and practice of martial arts. This concept applies not only to martial arts as every field has mental, physical, and motivational aspects.

Although Mind-Body-Spirit may appear straight forward it can be interpreted by the human mind differently. A martial arts teacher or organization can have a different order of importance, place more emphasis or have another interpretation on one aspect or another. The reality is that even if analyzed separately they are developed simultaneously.

I list *Spirit* third because as a teacher I find that students already have a level of enthusiasm or spirit when they begin training in martial arts. To learn a student needs to engage their *Mind* to connect with, and then begin to control their *Body* before infusing additional energy from their *Spirit.*

Some elements used to develop the martial arts spirit may not be interesting or understood by beginners, so those benefits can evolve in time. Too much energetic spirit at the beginning of training can get in the way of the mind being calm enough to learn and understand what the body is developing.

Some people feel uncomfortable with the term "Spirit" as they fear a religious inference other than their own faith. Spirit in the martial arts context does not refer to the Holy Spirit, although that is a phenomenon fully capable of moving the spirit, nor does it refer to any Eastern religious philosophy or belief system.

Even though the spirit referenced in martial arts training is not the religious spirit there are many religious people who have and do practice, and have evolved martial arts, and some who even preach when they teach. However, aside from individual beliefs and practices, religion is not a part of the martial arts matrix.

The *Spirit* in this martial arts context is used as a noun with the definition being the "non-physical part of a person that is the seat of emotions and character." Spirit under this definition is divided into two approaches that we seek to positively develop through martial arts training.

—

1) "The attitude or intentions with which someone undertakes or regards something." This is the inward motivation that drives us to reach our goals. It's how we approach an activity, the way we affect our environment through our behavior, and how much "heart" we put into something. This is felt as the passion and focus we put into that effort, our internal drive or fire, our will, determination, motivation, and inspiration.

2) "The vital principle or animating force within living things." This is the outward energy and enthusiasm we bring to an activity. A martial artist would bring his "fighting spirit" to a competition or test, have enthusiasm when working out or participating in a class. This is the strong energetic spirit needed to get through a real-life fight or other major life challenges.

Personal life events can lift our spirits, touch our hearts, or drive us towards a goal. This passionate human spirit can be seen displayed through speaking, singing, playing music, literature, art, dance, acting, and martial arts. Whether observed or experienced these can move us emotionally by touching our spirit, and we also can give this to others.

Most would agree that without a passionate spirit life would be dull, boring, uninspired, and spiritless. Life is felt and lived to the fullest when we feel passion and can share it with others. This passionate spirit makes human life unique and worthwhile.

What infuses the human spirit has many origins including the complicated human ego and timeless wisdom. Historically, "traditional" martial arts strive to direct and evolve the spirit with methods to develop individual character traits. These include *Honesty, Humility, Courtesy, Integrity, Self-Control, Perseverance, Determination,* and an *Indomitable Spirit.*

These important traits are developed and managed through discipline, structure, respect, tradition, formality, ritual, control, rules, and etiquette. In my students training manuals I put an acronym I created using the word CHARACTER, mostly as a reference for parents but also a good reminder for adults of these positive human character traits.

CHARACTER
Courtesy – Polite behavior towards others
Humility – Not intimidating or overwhelming others
Attitude – Positive disposition and acting in a friendly manner
Respect – Consideration (family, friends, authority, acquaintances)
Accomplishment – Mindset towards goal setting and attainment
Courage – Demonstrating integrity, confidence, and leadership qualities
Truthfulness – Practicing honesty and forthrightness
Etiquette – Not making others feel uncomfortable, having good manners
Responsibility – Maturity that accepts and completes tasks

This necessity to help in the overall development of a person's character makes the traditional martial arts approach uniquely special to the overall development of a student. These traditions are intangibles forming a foundation that makes martial arts more than just about fighting.

The ancients knew and viewed these as necessary for anyone to fully benefit from physical martial arts training and the responsibility this knowledge brings. They knew a long time ago what the Spiderman character discovered that "with great power comes great responsibility."

Martial arts skill is a power that can be acquired and developed but that comes with an obligation to not abuse that power while trying to make a positive contribution to society and do good when possible. For centuries martial art teachers have recognized their responsibility in helping students develop these attributes and to help them develop into well-rounded and mature people.

The martial arts tradition of discipline, structure, respect, formality, ritual, control, rules, and etiquette are used with the goal of developing a skilled practitioner with a controlled and motivated spirit. This is the bigger picture of martial arts training developed through more than just the concepts and principles of fighting and physical technique.

It also creates an appreciation for tradition and the benefits that many ancient methods can still contribute to modern cultures. Technology may change but the human spirit with its emotions and desires are the same since the beginning of human time. Others have been observing and figuring this out for thousands of years so only the foolish and the arrogant would ignore this wisdom.

This intention to develop the human spirit increases internal strength and personal power. Humility then grows with an increased awareness that many have gone before us, and a recognition of the timeless value of ancient wisdom as it is passed forward.

Together, these help in developing a positive, harmonious, humble and enthusiastic *Spirit* for life; balanced with an intelligent focused *Mind* and a healthy trained *Body*. Martial arts can, at its best, be a powerful tool for developing the human spirit to its fullest potential.

MARTIAL ARTS TRADITION
Chapter 11

Many in martial arts use a group of traditions that evolved through the Asian martial arts, often with modifications for language and culture. They are used for practical reasons and to develop an individual not only in martial arts but to build character and improve their humanity.

Some of these elements are present in the military structure as well where they are used for discipline and character building, something needed when teaching someone how to cause harm. Technology changes but human emotion, thought, and desire has always and will always be the same.

Many parents have heard of the character building qualities inherent in martial arts training prompting many to enroll their children in programs with the hope that their children will develop these qualities. The formalities and traditions inherent in martial arts are a major part of that development.

Most parents "get it" and have faith in the big picture benefit of the traditional martial arts method, although some may just want their kids to learn to fight or learn some self-defense. The traditional way takes time but will eventually have a great and positive influence on a person's life.

My observation running a facility where traditional karate classes are taught in one area and non-traditional gym workout classes in another is that those who opt out of the entire martial arts experience don't stay as long or benefit as greatly. Most dabble then become bored and drift away long before their traditional martial art counterparts.

Traditional program students, many who also do gym training, stay much longer and gain an infinitely greater amount of physical knowledge along with emotional and personal strength. People choose their own paths however and if attaining a Black Belt were easy then everyone would have one, which obviously would make it not be as valuable or meaningful.

In any case, the fact that all older martial arts styles have these traditions to some degree makes a compelling case for their benefit. Things evolve for a reason and the longevity of many traditional martial arts methods demonstrates a line of succession supporting the evolution of their use.

The benefits of structure and behavior standards should therefore not be ignored or discarded. Anyone who believes they know more or has figured out something nobody in the history of humanity before them has discovered shows arrogance of epic proportions. Reinventing the wheel and ignoring lessons learned by people and cultures before our time is foolish.

Here's a summary of traditions that I use followed by explanations as to why.

Creeds, Pledges and/or Oaths are a tradition that helps practitioners understand their responsibilities as they acquire skill and knowledge. They are statements of purpose that guide and help build a sound mental approach as to when fighting is a righteous act and to provide moral direction. These have also been statements of alliance, although that seems less prevalent in our culture.

Symbols are a tradition used to associate with an organization or a martial art style. These can be powerful visuals that give a sense of belonging while providing mental strength and inspiration through that association. They can generate respect, or even intimidate and instill fear of the person wearing the symbol of an organization, gang, or style. Most have multiple meanings built into the shape, color and design. Symbols include patches, crests, flags, banners, tattoos, etc.

Etiquette and Rules of Conduct is important in martial arts training as they play a significant role in the environment where people meet to practice. Camaraderie often builds in these environments making it a social outlet where lifelong friendships often develop.

Formal Behavior demonstrates respect for each other, the training environment, and those who have come before us. Showing respect for teachers and fellow students is at the very least important for everyone's safety. These polite displays often develop into life habits outside the martial arts environment that can bring civility, soften tense environments, and make hostile societal interaction less likely. Bowing or addressing a classmate or instructor as Sir, Mam, Mr., Ms., Sensei, Sifu, Coach, etc. are all ways that demonstrate this respect.

Ceremony and Ritual is how people are recognized and advanced. In martial arts these have evolved over generations and are adjusted to fit culture and personal preference. These gatherings of supportive people give strength and power to all involved in their common alliance.

Rank or acknowledgement of advancement based upon accomplishment and seniority is an essential element to the overall benefit attained through martial arts. Confidence is reassured through this process with recognition and status awarded based upon effort and achievement.

Organizations and instructors may have a different take on these traditions but the essence and goal of providing guidance, developing character, and providing a social anchor are the same. Society then benefits from this in a way not provided by unstructured activities. They help to make martial arts a true unselfish gift to a culture and humanity.

CREEDS, PLEDGES & OATHS

A belief system has evolved out of the oriental martial arts tradition that requires and demands discipline, respect, and a determined spirit towards life, death, and the skill of fighting. These have manifested in Kenpo as the Kenpo Karate Creed, various Belt Rank Pledges, and a Black Belt Oath.

Stating one's intention is important, so I require students memorize and recite a "Creed" for Yellow Belt, then a "Pledge" at their various belt ranks through my system, and eventually a Black Belt "Oath" as part of the testing process. I also have required pledges for 2nd and 3rd Degree Black Belt.

Kenpo, like many traditional martial arts, teaches more than just fighting and these important statements give students a level appropriate reference and reason to understand important and valuable lessons surrounding the use of their skills, along with societal interaction guidelines.

Below are the Creed, Pledges, and Oath I use through 3rd Degree Black Belt, many of which are modified versions of what I inherited from American Kenpo founder Edmund Parker and my longtime instructor Jim Mitchell. I authored some pledges where none existed before and have included some historical context during the time I saw these evolving.

Jim Mitchell was an Ed Parker student, featured prominently in Mr. Parker's Book 2 doing the stance work, and is responsible for naming most of the Pledges I use in my system. He authored a few and modified others, primarily for trademark reasons according to him after becoming no longer affiliated with Mr. Parker in the early 1980's.

Below are the versions used at my school followed by Mr. Parkers version, where one existed, and then Mr. Mitchell's version below, if it applies. This will put the pledges I use in perspective with explanations as to modifications or additions.

The Creed
A "Creed" transcends the style through each belt rank and level, with its purpose to give a focus as to the reason for developing the knowledge. Kenpo is a street self-defense art, so the creed tells about our style, our purpose for training, and the terms under which we would use our skills.

Kenpo Karate Creed: (Yellow Belt)
I come to you with Kenpo Karate, the law of the fist and the empty hand. Should I be forced to defend myself, my family or my friends; my principles or my honor; should it be a matter of life or death, of right or wrong; then here are my weapons, Kenpo Karate, the law of the fist and the empty hand.

Edmund K Parker's Original Creed:
"I come to you with only Karate, empty hands. I have no weapons, but should I be forced to defend myself, my principles or my honor, should it be a matter of life or death, of right or wrong; then here are my weapons, karate, my empty hands."

Jim Mitchell's modified Version:
"I come to you with Kenpo Karate, the law of the fist and the empty hand. My skills include fighting with or without weapons. Should I be forced to defend myself, my family or my friends: My principles or my honor; should it be a matter of life or death, of right or wrong; then here are my weapons, Kenpo Karate, the law of the fist and the empty hand.

Mr. Mitchell added "fighting with or without weapons" and to defend "my family or my friends" plus he added "Kenpo" before Karate and "the law of the fist" to clarify the term Kenpo Karate.

I removed his 2nd sentence, "My skills include fighting with or without weapons", as it was not accurate to imply external weapon training as a major component of Kenpo, especially for beginners learning and reciting this creed. It also limits advanced Kenpo practitioners by ignoring the Mind as the ultimate weapon we always have with us. "Then here are my weapons" leaves it all available to interpretation.

Pledges
A "Pledge" in martial arts passes on moral lessons. Since it would be difficult to cover every character quality in a short *Creed,* the *Pledges* give an opportunity to provide additional guidance over time.

Pledge of Understanding: (Orange Belt)
I understand that I am taking the first steps in mastering a unique and powerful art and that to complete my journey I must dedicate my training to those who have traveled the path before me, these include my instructors, the current and past masters of our system and other Black Belts.

Edmund K Parker's Original Orange Belt Pledge:
"I understand that I am but a beginner in a new and fascinating art that will direct me to greater obligations and responsibilities. To honor my obligations and responsibilities I pledge myself to serve my instructors, fellow students, and fellow men."

Jim Mitchell's Modified Version:
"I understand that I have taken but the first step in mastering a unique and powerful art, and that to complete my journey I must dedicate myself to those who have trod the path before me, namely our masters, other Black Belts and my instructors."

My version is a modified version of Mr. Mitchell's modified version. Mr. Parker's original pledge spoke to obligations, responsibilities, and serving, perhaps a reflection of his religious upbringing.

I felt that Mr. Mitchell's modified version was more eloquent and better written but a couple of my students early on seemed uncomfortable with the line "I must dedicate myself..." as some were Christians and told me they dedicate their lives to God, not to any man or group. I agreed and did not want students to dedicate themselves to me but to their training.

Pledge of Restraint: (Purple Belt)
I pledge solemnly and on my honor that I will never misuse my skills to hurt or make afraid. I will fight only if forced to defend myself. I will be slow to anger and take offense, and quick to forgive and forget personal affront.

Edmund K Parker's Original Purple Belt Pledge:
"I hold the Art of Kenpo Karate sacred and freely take upon myself the obligation and responsibility that I shall never misuse my skill to hurt or make afraid. I shall fight only if forced to defend myself and shall be slow to anger, loathe to take offense, quick to forgive and forget personal affront."

Jim Mitchell's Modified Version:
"I pledge solemnly and on my honor that I shall never misuse my skills in Kenpo Karate to hurt or make afraid. Fighting shall be for the purpose of self-defense only. I shall be slow to anger and take offense; and quick to forgive and forget personal affront."

As you can see they are all very close with minor changes on emphasis, phrasing and punctuation choices but the essence is the same.

Pledge of Defense: (Blue Belt)
I shall never let pride rule my passions and will defend with all the skill I possess the weak, the helpless and the oppressed. I shall come forth with all of my abilities to defend my fellow man in time of need, regardless of race, religion, or creed.

Edmund K Parker's Original Blue Belt Pledge
"I shall never let pride rule my passions and will defend, with all the skill I possess, the weak, the helpless, and the oppressed. I pledge an unswerving loyalty to the association and my instructor, in addition I pledge an unending effort to earn the self-same loyalty from those who look to me for training."

Jim Mitchell's Modified Version:
"I shall never let pride rule my passions and will defend with all the skill I possess the weak, the helpless and the oppressed. I shall come forth with all my abilities to defend my fellow man in time of need, regardless of race, religion or creed."

My pledge is identical to Mr. Mitchell's version of Mr. Parker's pledge with the addition of an "of" for grammatical reasons. Mr. Mitchell took the two loyalty ideas proposed in Mr. Parker's Blue Belt Pledge and created what he used as his Green Belt pledge and what I use at Red Belt, after Green.

Pledge of Accomplishment: (Green Belt)

I pledge that through persistence and determination I will continue to sharpen my skills, increase my knowledge and broaden my horizons. My skill will be tempered in the fire of my will. My sweat will be the cologne of my accomplishment. I pledge an unending effort to accomplish the levels of skill as set forth by my instructors and my school.

Edmund K Parker's Original Green Belt Pledge

"I pledge a continued effort to sharpen my skills, to increase my knowledge and to broaden my horizons. I shall obligate myself under the direction of my instructor to learn the skills of a teacher, which will enable me to teach my skills in the prescribed manner outlined by Mr. Parker."

Jim Mitchell's Original Green Belt Pledge

(This became the outline for my Red Belt "Pledge of Loyalty")
"I pledge an unswerving loyalty to those from whom I receive the art of Kenpo Karate. To prove my loyalty, I pledge myself to train diligently in the art, for my studio and my association. Should my loyalty be tested I shall never waiver from the path that our master has shown me."

In Jim Mitchell's school when I was there we had an Advanced Green Belt rank (Green with Brown Stripes), that I have replaced with a Red Belt. In either case we needed a Pledge for that rank, so Jim Mitchell wrote his own "Pledge of Loyalty", taken from the second half of Mr. Parker's Blue Belt Pledge, and put it on the lower Green Belt list. He then wrote his Pledge of Accomplishment and used it for the higher Green Belt rank.

Pledge of Loyalty: (Red Belt)

I pledge never to take lightly the loyalty and trust that I share with my teachers in Kenpo. I will strive to attain and share that same loyalty and trust in my dealings with others inside and outside of the Karate School. I resolve that the loyalty and trust I give is not based upon an expected return but upon what is right to give.

Mr. Parker did not have a pledge or a belt rank at this level.

Jim Mitchell's Original Advanced Green Belt Pledge

(His version of Mr. Parkers Green Belt Pledge that I modified for Green)
"I pledge a continued effort to sharpen my skills, to increase my knowledge and to broaden my horizons. I shall temper my skills in the fire of my will; my sweat shall be the cologne of my accomplishment. I pledge an unending effort to accomplish the levels of skill that are set forth by my instructor and the World Kenpo Karate Association." (The WKKA was Mr. Mitchell's association).

—

I use my version of this pledge at Green Belt with the first sentence similar to the first sentence of Mr. Mitchell's original Green Belt Pledge. The rest of my version is the philosophical expression of Lao Zi's quote from the Tao Te Ching, "The sage has no mind of his own, He is good to people who are good. He is also good to people who are not good, because essence is goodness."

Instructors Pledge (3rd Class Brown)
I pledge that I will obligate myself under the direction of my instructor to learn the skills of a teacher. I will strive to demonstrate an attitude of respect and appreciation for my students, my teachers and the teachings of Kenpo Karate. I promise to guide others toward an understanding of the responsibility that this knowledge entails. I make this pledge solemnly and on my honor.

Edmund K Parker's Original Instructors Pledge
"I pledge that as my skill as a teacher progresses I will never condemn, ridicule, embarrass or shame any student or fellow instructor in the presence of a class or group. All grievances or disputes shall be conducted in private away from group observation."

Jim Mitchell's Instructors Pledge
"I solemnly pledge that I will obligate myself under the direction of my instructor to learn the skills of a teacher, which will enable me to teach those students assigned to my care. I will treat with respect both my teachers and my students. The welfare of my students will be my first consideration. I will strive to impart to my students an attitude of respect and appreciation for the teachings of Kenpo Karate and an understanding of the responsibility that a knowledge of Kenpo Karate entails. I make this pledge solemnly and on my honor."

Mr. Mitchell did not use Mr. Parker's pledge, and it seems to reflect a time where an admonition about condemning and ridiculing in public must have been necessary. This is all conjecture as it was before my time and I never discussed it with Mr. Parker or Mr. Mitchell. However, reading Mr. Parker's pledges takes one back to a different time and attitude in martial arts. My contribution to this pledge was to shorten Mr. Mitchell's version by eliminating redundancies and fixing grammar.

Pledge of Respect (2nd Class Brown Belt)
I pledge to treat others with courtesy and respect at all times whether inside or outside of the Karate School. I understand that the courtesy and respect I give may not always be returned to me equally but that my obligation as a trained martial artist and a good citizen is to act as a role model for others by demonstrating correct behavior at all times.

Edmund K Parker's 2nd Brown Pledge
"I understand that like a doctor, the private affairs of students and fellow instructors that come to my attention during the exercising of my responsibilities are privileged communications and must never be discussed with any living soul. I vow that I will never violate this pledge nor any other for the sake of personal benefit."

I was not required to learn a pledge at this rank and I did not see the need for the pledge Mr. Parker used. I felt a "Pledge of Respect" was needed so I wrote the one I use at this level to reiterate the Lao Zi lesson quoted in the Red Belt Pledge but also to echo Paul's quote from Ephesians 4:29 "Do not let unwholesome talk come out of your mouths, but only what is helpful for building others up according to their needs, that it may benefit those who listen" (I prefer this version although other Bible versions can word the same sentiments slightly differently).

Pledge of Determination (Advanced Brown Belt)
As I look forward to the next milestone in my training I hereby pledge to reaffirm my will and determination to accomplish my goals. These qualities of success have helped me reach this point in my training and will continue to motivate me to reach and exceed my personal expectations in this and in all things.

Edmund K Parker's 1st Class Brown Belt Pledge
"I honor and hold sacred the right of all men to protect themselves. I further hold that as a trained martial artist in Kenpo Karate I will take upon myself all obligations and responsibilities deemed sacred to my family, God, country, and association."

During my time with Mr. Mitchell I was not required to learn a pledge at this rank. I did not use Mr. Parker's pledge as the basis for my 1st Brown pledge as I felt a "Pledge of Determination" was needed at this level but I do use a small part of it in my Black Belt Oath.

Black Belt Oath (1st Degree Black Belt)
I pledge that my search for knowledge will never cease. I will strive to act with courtesy and respect, always searching for peaceful resolution. I will be honest and forthright in my dealings with others. My word will be my bond, my handshake my oath of friendship and trust. If ever forced to violence I will fight the good and righteous fight, always bearing in mind my obligations, responsibilities, and loyalty to God, my family, my country, and my friends. By honoring this sacred vow, I make myself worthy to join the ranks of the Kenpo Black Belt.

Edmund K Parker's 1st Black Pledge
"I hold that my time and my skill are the assets to my profession, assets which grow in value as I progress in the art until as a 3rd dan, I stand as a fully qualified instructor. It shall also be my responsibility to protect any students from ravenous individuals who would try to take advantage of personal weaknesses to divest the gullible into unprofitable paths, to preserve the sacred things, family, God and country, I pledge my all."

During my time Mr. Mitchell did not require a Black Belt Pledge. I rewrote this pledge to reflect the value system I wanted expressed, but I liked the order of importance I recall Mr. Mitchell stating which was God then family, country, friends. All of this could be debated but that is the order I decided to use in what I call the "Black Belt Oath." Oath rather than Pledge as it is a more powerful level of commitment and intent.

Regarding the order of importance, it is open for debate and could be a long philosophical discussion, but for my mind I agreed with Mr. Mitchell that our relationship with God (whatever comprehended to mean) is primary and transcends our entire life. God is always present even if family is not around.

Family comes next because they are the closest relationship to our existence. Family dynamic aside this placement represents those that we have as our closest connection to life. Then country followed by friends.

I realize in a tyrannical form of government our friends would probably come first as we fight that government, but in our constitutional republic we all buy into the concept and role of our government, flawed as it may be. Therefore, country comes first as we would not, under "normal" circumstances, support our friends to violently overthrow the government. Ok, that was deep and could be a lively discussion with varied opinions and different takes. Hey, it's America.

Pledge of Commitment (2nd Black)
I pledge to be goal-oriented and resolute for myself and for the good of those that I can affect. I pledge to be result oriented with a firm conviction to affect the world in a positive way. I pledge to be forward thinking yet content with today but not satisfied with tomorrow.

I never saw any creeds, pledges, or oaths beyond 1st Black Belt during my time in Mr. Parkers IKKA (International Kenpo Karate Association) or Mr. Mitchell's WKKA (World Kenpo Karate Association).

The pledge I use here was written by me with the purpose of addressing commitment and intention, which I felt had not been stated previously in a pledge. I wanted to help the 1st Degree Black Belts now working on 2nd Degree realize that attaining 1st Black was merely the beginning of their martial arts journey.

I wanted them to still have goals and realize the affect they have on those around them due to not only their status as Black Belts but because the type of student who gets to this rank generally are, or become, leaders that others look to for guidance and motivation. I also wanted them to affirm being happy with their lives but not content to just rest on their laurels. All these thoughts are reflected in the 2nd Degree Black Belt Pledge.

Pledge of Honor (3rd Black)
I pledge on my honor to live up the expectations and guidelines set forth by the code of the modern warrior. I will be a polite contributor to the society of which I am a part. I am honored to walk in the footsteps of past great contributors to this noble discipline. I will strive to be worthy of future appreciation.

Again, I never saw any creeds, pledges, or oaths past 1st Black during my time in Mr. Parkers IKKA (International Kenpo Karate Association) or Mr. Mitchell's WKKA (World Kenpo Karate Association).

In my system the curriculum ends at 3rd Degree Black Belt so even though many Black Belts still attend Belt Tests and Special Events there is tendency to not attend class as often as before. In addition, I have always encouraged my students to study other arts as I felt it all would make their Kenpo better, and many have done so.

I also wanted this level of student to begin thinking about his or her own legacies in martial arts. My intention was to give those wanting to become 3rd Degree Black Belts a vision of their place in the big picture and to see themselves as role models and future contributors to the arts.

THE POWER OF SYMBOLS

The human mind has a powerful attachment to symbols. These affect the spirit and are often used in martial arts as banners, crests, patches, tattoos, etc. The Yin Yang symbol is the most enduring of the 3 samples shown here with the Ed Parker IKKA patch the most commonly used Kenpo patch. Included is my own American Kenpo Alliance (AKA) patch with description as a reference for the symbolism in a symbol.

Well-known Martial Arts Symbols
Chinese Yin Yang Symbol
&
The Ed Parker IKKA Crest

AKA Patch Meanings

Equilateral Triangle Shape
3 training pillars: Mind=Open Palms; Body=Fist inside Open Hand; Spirit=Hands Praying
3 life goals: Peace=Open Palms; Control=Fist inside Open Hand; Harmony=Hands Praying
3 corners open inside: Trust=Open Palms; Cooperation=Fist inside Open Hand; Togetherness=Hands Praying
3 sharp edges point outward to repel attack
Triangle within a triangle for 3-dimensional awareness of zones and angles

Yin Yang Symbol
Traces the Chinese roots of our Kenpo system - Represents an eternal search for balance and harmony - Shows the circular system hidden within the linear system - White Dot for focus - Black Dot for awareness - Yin within Yang and Yang within Yin.

Three Hand Positions
Traces the Japanese roots of our Kenpo system - Both palms facing out show no weapons (peace) - Fist inside folded palm indicates not abusing our power (control) - Praying hands represents the spiritual nature of man (harmony).

Words
KEN PO – "Fist Law" (Law of the Fist) shows Chinese Lineage (Chuan Fa), Circular within Linear
KARA TE - "Empty Hand" shows Japanese Lineage, Linear within Circular
AMERICAN - Free Thinking, Individualistic, Open Minded, Progressive
KENPO - Linguistic spelling with an "N" the way Mr. Parker wanted it
ALLIANCE - Shows camaraderie with other practitioners

Colors
RED: Blood represents Family holding our art, society, and all of us together
WHITE: Purity - the Beginning Level of Training yet the Highest Level of Natural Knowledge
BLACK: Experience - the Highest Level of Training yet the Beginning Level of Actual Knowledge

---

ETIQUETTE AND BEHAVIOR

These are statements of decorum and manners among participants in a martial arts facility. They are important for many reasons, among which is participant safety and for viability of the business or club. Without some guidance negative actions and attitudes can develop which could destroy the camaraderie of a group.

Below are the rules of "Etiquette and Behavior" I use at my school as an example, with a follow up explanation for clarification purposes.

1. Bow-In facing the *Training Area* when entering and Bow-Out facing the *Training Area* when leaving.

Bowing is a traditional formality to show respect. We bow into and out of the area where martial arts skill is learned to show earned respect for current and especially former practitioners, instructors, and martial arts masters who trained in these environments.

The spirit and memory of former practitioners is appreciated and in many cases their efforts gave us the baseline we study and that allows us to learn while continuing to develop and evolve what they left us to develop an even higher knowledge base, and we hope future generations will show respect for our efforts and contributions in this same way.

2. No shoes, jewelry, or gum chewing allowed in class. Wear shoes from outside to avoid tracking dirt and debris onto the training floor. Wash your workout clothes frequently enough to avoid excessive body odor. Keep feet clean with finger and toenails clipped.

Most traditional martial arts settings train in bare feet for weapon development, safety, and to minimize wear and tear to the training floor while not tracking debris in from outside as this is also the surface every part of the body may interact with. Bare feet are also universal as compared with the different footwear that could be worn. This makes it more consistent when teaching or learning how to form and use various parts of the feet for kicking, pivoting, or when doing footwork.

Jewelry is unsafe in the training environment as it can result in injury, or become damaged, or damage equipment. Gum is a choking hazard or can fall out onto the training floor surface and become a nuisance.

Good hygiene is important as it is uncomfortable and unsanitary to train with people who stink, so emphasis is made to encourage cleanliness inside and out. Long fingernails can snag, get torn off, scratch training partners, or become damaged. It can also be difficult to make a fist and grasp with long nails.

3. While in class the male students wear their belt knot on their left hip, female students on their right hip. Instructors wear their belt knot in the middle. Do not wear your belt in public except for demonstrations or tournaments.

This is traditional in many Kenpo schools as inherited from Kung Fu. It shows respect and humility when a student is in a class setting. This is done at all levels so when a 1st Degree Black Belt is teaching they wear their belt knot in the middle, and when in class their belt knot is moved to the side. Everyone wears their belt knot in the middle for tournaments, demonstrations, ceremonies, and presentations.

4. Instructors, Coaches, Trainers, and other students are to be treated with respect at all times. Address teachers formally while in the studio and in class (Mr., Mrs., Ms., Sensei, Sifu, Coach, etc). Follow their directions but also feel free to ask questions if you do not understand.

The people who teach us in life deserve respect and should be acknowledged in a respectful manner. Many may not ask for it directly but that does not take away from the fact they have spent a considerable amount of time learning a skill they are now willing to pass on to you. The least a student can do is show respect for these people and their efforts to pass it forward.

5. When your class is asked to "Line up" say "Yes Sir" or "Yes Mam" and do so quickly. Classes will line up in belt ranking order with senior students closer to the front and to the right. New students line up in the back and to the left. When class is dismissed, say "Thank You Sir" or "Thank You Mam." If you come in late, go to the instructor leading the class and ask permission to join the class.

The hierarchy of the class allows for those who have achieved a higher rank to line up closer to the front. Common courtesy, good manners, along with safety and the teachers lesson plan dictates that if you are late then requesting permission or waiting for acknowledgement and direction to join the class is appropriate, polite, and practical.

6. Do not lean against the walls, fold your arms, cross your legs while standing, or put your hands on your hips while in the training facility.

This list of postures could all be interpreted as forms of disinterest, laziness, boredom, and disrespect for the learning environment and the teacher. In addition, leaning against the walls makes them dirty and unsanitary, which increases the school's maintenance costs and can become an eye sore.

7. Do not have unnecessary conversations during class.

The focus, attention, and intention while in a class must be on the task at hand. It is impolite and unsafe to distract, and become distracted with discussions, while a teacher is explaining or while people arc training, and unrelated conversations are never acceptable while in class.

8. Show courtesy and respect towards others at all times in and out of the training area.

When learning fighting skill especially it is important that courtesy and respect are at the forefront as a bad or disrespectful attitude can have negative consequences. Everyone can then train hard while still feeling psychologically comfortable and physically unthreatened.

9. Do not boast about your skills and never talk badly about someone else's training facility, instructors, coaches, skill, or abilities.

Whatever the skill, talent, or accomplishment level of a practitioner it is never right to brag or boast as it diminishes your efforts. Be humble and accept compliments directed towards you gracefully. Criticizing others, whether true or not, reflects badly on the person doing the talking and on their school.

10. The martial arts skills you are learning are to be used for self-defense or sport purposes only. Your obligation as a martial arts practitioner in a civil society is to stay away from physical altercation, unless <u>forced</u> to defend yourself, your family, or others who cannot defend themselves.

A fight under any circumstances can be extremely dangerous for everyone involved regardless of skill level. There are times in life where it may be a necessary choice within the guidelines of being "forced to fight." Competing in a sport fighting event however is an acceptable outlet for testing one's martial art skills.

RULES OF CONDUCT

These rules help maintain order in a class setting.

Below are the "Rules of Conduct" I use at my school as an example, with a follow up explanation for clarification purposes.

1. Be on time and ready to begin class promptly.

This shows respect for the teacher and classmates while allowing each class to begin when it is scheduled and helps to develop good life habits.

2. Check in before class begins.

Signing or scanning in is used for attendance and billing records.

3. Do not use any of the school's equipment without permission.

It is impolite to use someone else's things without their permission, plus it is unsafe to use something you may not have been shown how to use properly. Check first, usually it will be ok.

4. A Brown or Black Belt Instructor must supervise free sparring, and full gear is required.

All contact sparring must be observed to assure safety. This includes wearing the proper equipment, agreeing to and staying within agreed upon rules of contact between participants. These are all important from a safety, legal, and training standpoint.

5. Groin protection is required for all students, male and female.

The groin is a primary target in self-defense arts like Kenpo so attacks to the groin are common with even sport fighting having a chance of groin contact. Men and women both react and feel pain when struck in the groin, so both must wear that protection.

6. Wear the proper uniform and belt while attending class. Uniform sleeves should not hang past the wrists or be above the bottom of the elbows. Uniform overlap top is left over right.

Uniformity is important for structure and discipline, with the traditional Japanese uniform (Gi) a functional part of training as it provides some sanitary separation between bodies and a contact cushion, along with handles for grabbing that allows for practice of many martial art techniques.

Sleeve and pant length partly reflects the instructors need to see the wrists and ankles, but also so as not interfere with the hands or causing the feet to trip. Left overlap on top is the traditional Japanese kimono wrap for the living and allows for the school's patch to be worn over the heart. The belt denotes level but also supports the back for heavy training.

FORMAL GREETINGS

Most martial arts schools encourage and may even require students observe certain formal greetings to attend. Most of these have been passed on from predecessors in the martial arts.

These common greetings are done for specific reasons, none of which are religious. There seems to be a fair amount of confusion and ignorance regarding martial arts formalities so here is an examination of *Bowing, Saluting, Meditating, Shaking Hands,* and *Addressing Formally.*

Bowing

Many cultures practice this form of respect, with bowing common in most Asian cultures but were also common in older Western cultures and are still present among royal classes where they exist.

Some interpret bowing as a form of worship while expressing sentiments like "I only worship God" and "I bow to no man." I would agree that only God should be worshipped but this argument misses the entire point and type of bowing being done. The martial arts bow is with the eyes up showing respect whereas the bow of worship is with the eyes down.

Civility in a society requires that we each demonstrate basic decorum and manners towards others. Otherwise animosities can build between people that could potentially lead to violence, so it is important to show respect in daily interactions. Traditions that accomplish this can be verbal like saying "hello," physical like shaking hands, or visual like smiling, saluting, and in some cultures and traditions, bowing.

In ancient times the act of bowing accomplished two other important tasks for people who wanted to show respect towards each other. It could be done a safe distance so as not to expose them to potential injury by an ill-intentioned person, unlike handshaking that is done with faith that the counterpart intends no harm.

The other benefit to bowing is that germs, bacteria, or illness are not transferred through body contact as can happen when shaking hands. That is why my mom, and probably yours too, told us to wash our hands often. Not touching other people's hands unnecessarily was and is a terrific way to keep diseases from spreading, and in past times before antibiotics, this was especially important.

Bowing into and out of the training floor is done to especially show respect and appreciation for the spirit and dedication of martial arts practitioners who have trained before us, living and dead. They passed through similar portals and gave their sweat, blood, and sometimes their lives to benefit themselves and others by training and contributing to the martial arts.

Without great practitioners of old passing this information forward the martial arts would not contain the base of knowledge currently available, which enables us to move forward without reinventing too many wheels. By *Bowing* we choose to show our sincere appreciation to their memory as we hope future generations of martial artists will appreciate our efforts as they enter and leave their training areas.

Saluting

This is a ceremonial method used when meeting, welcoming, or formally addressing others. Members of the U.S. military will salute each other by placing a stiff right hand next to the right side of their head. Martial artists also salute or perform a salutation of some type. Short greetings like the praying hands used by Muay Thai practitioners or the closed right fist wrapped inside a left palm done by Kenpo and Kung Fu practitioners are common.

There are also longer formal greetings like the Wai Khru done before a Muay Thai fight or the combination greeting of Kenpo we refer to as the "Salute" and "Greeting" that demonstrate our Kenpo lineage. The "Salute" shows the Chinese Shaolin Temple lineage that our art inherited from Professor William Chow, who was Ed Parker's instructor. Our "Greeting" shows the Japanese Ko Sho Ryu Kempo lineage that our art inherited from James Mitose, who was one of William Chow's instructors.

Since the physical art is universal these salutes are also a practical statement that crosses language barriers to show the type of martial art we study. Others in martial arts, regardless of culture and language, can in this way know what you study by the salute you present to them.

Meditating

The word "meditation" essentially means to think and focus intently on something either externally or internally and is something that everyone does at some level.

At the beginning of each class we meditate *(i.e. focus our intention)* into our breath, our posture, our rooted feet, and to learning and training in martial arts. It is important that we focus on where we are and what we are doing in these moments to be fully engaged so we can fully benefit from the experience.

Someone who is not focused in that moment or is not concentrating could get injured or injure someone else. Therefore, meditating to draw focus to our current activity is designed to engage the mind, body, and spirit into the present. The same is done at the end of class to reflect and absorb lessons learned and practiced, while also giving closure to the activity.

Shaking Hands

As mentioned, shaking hands is potentially dangerous because it is a good faith offering to someone who could easily take advantage of this vulnerable gesture. In a strange way this is also a good reason to shake hands as it shows faith and trust in others.

This is also an expected custom in Western culture upon meeting or greeting someone showing friendship and respect. It would be regarded as rudeness to refuse to shake an outstretched hand.

Personally, I like shaking hands because it energizes a greeting and brings people closer together through the contact. Many times, the opposite hand is placed on the back of the other persons hand as a reaffirming sign of respect, caring, or to show closeness to that person. We must really notice someone to shake his or her hand, and everyone wants to be noticed and appreciated. Shaking hands is one way to show that.

The three main methods used in Western culture to shake hands are the "traditional" shake where palms are clasped together with the thumbs over the hand webbing, the "soul" shake where the thumbs are interlocked with the palms together, also the starting hand position for arm wrestling, and the "Indian" shake where the wrist and forearm are grasped. All are acceptable in the right context.

Depending on the time and place a shoulder bump and perhaps a free hand back pat is often an acceptable add on. High fives, fist bumps, etc., are other less formal greeting often used as signs of encouragement or congratulations.

Addressing Formally

This is how we show respect for others by referring to anyone in a formal social setting as sir or mam, or by acknowledging someone's title or status in various environments (Doctor, Professor, Sensei, Sifu, Mr., Ms., Mrs., etc.)

This practice instantly sets the tone as one of respect and courtesy while bringing down potential stress. It is a good and customary practice, that martial artists are often expected to do, that then becomes a life habit with many side benefits.

TESTING & RANK

A vital component of any learning process involves being tested. This applies to learning at every level from grade school through college, and in other environments as well, like martial arts. When we are tested preparation is required so effort is put forth to internalize the knowledge being tested on.

For the martial artist this testing process can come in many forms from planned to unexpected. Planned or voluntary methods of testing can include testing for a new belt color where passing results in a higher rank. Testing can also take place in the competition environment against others who are also testing themselves. Unexpected tests can and probably will come up in life, so these can be a measure of how we have progressed and react under pressure.

With voluntary testing there is time for planning and preparation. This expectation of testing ourselves often causes stress because we have time to think about what is coming up. Learning how to handle and manage that stressful energy is part of the testing and growing process.

I have found it useful for myself to reframe my mindset by changing the terms used to describe those feelings. For example, I would not say or think that "I am nervous or afraid" of an upcoming test, competition, or demonstration, but that "I am anxious and excited."

Life's unexpected tests leave little time for planning and preparation. Sometimes we are prepared based upon training to handle an unexpected real-life experience but other times we may just have to "wing it" and hope that we have good instincts, and perhaps some luck.

A crucial part of any real-life test is in the acceptance this is really happening to us as denial can be dangerous in these circumstances. The stakes can be much higher, creating a heightened level of adrenaline and focus is present that must be channeled.

For military and law enforcement it may not be as surprising and may occur after some preparation, but for most people a street altercation or criminal assault catches them off guard.

Reflection comes later but a key attribute needed to get through any test is a sense of competitiveness. This desire to win whether from pride, a desire to prove something to our self or others, a need to survive, or just not wanting to lose are powerful driving forces. These come from our ego and if strong will not let us be defeated mentally and will push us forward towards success and victory.

Since there is no way to prepare for every possible unexpected test life can and will throw at us the focus here is on voluntary ways of being tested in martial arts. These contribute in our ability to deal with the unexpected as experience and increased awareness gives us confidence and maturity to deal with, avoid, or nullify something before it occurs.

Traditional martial arts use belt testing, so students can demonstrate new levels of proficiency, but also to give them an opportunity to perform under pressure. Whether through belt testing or competition these stressful situations build character and raise a person's effective skill level by requiring full focus and effort.

Some people prefer the great fitness aspects of martial arts training so practice it as a hobby with no real personal growth goal in mind. They prefer to avoid curriculum and testing as those require work outside of class and add stress to what may already be a stressful life, job, School, etc.

Sport styles like Boxing, Kickboxing, Wrestling, and MMA generally don't have belt levels so the testing available is acquired through competing. My observation in running a gym is that many people who train in sport styles but are not competing lose their enthusiasm long before their curriculum and competition-based counterparts.

With the only reward for training being conditioning, technique refinement, and perhaps the social interaction the novelty can wear off more quickly. To stay motivated competition is recommended for those training in a sport style, or as a supplement with a traditional style.

Sport competition is one of the best ways to test oneself as stress comes from many uncontrollable factors. A competition often takes place away from the normal training environment and usually against people who are not regular training partners. They are uncooperative and trying to defeat you to win for themselves and their school or gym.

To beat them requires competitive drive and a determined desire to win that must match and probably exceed theirs. It requires engaging the competitive spirit, acquired skill, developed conditioning, and strong will, all while blocking out whatever pressure was felt beforehand. Competition along with curriculum-based testing and even demonstrations provide great personal growth and learning opportunities.

Curriculum-based martial arts include ongoing learning, increased knowledge, progressive recognition, and acknowledged accomplishment. These provide continued motivation to train as one of life's biggest success secrets is in just showing up. This process keeps more people showing up.

To become the best that you can be at anything it is imperative to have or find ways to be tested and challenge yourself. Martial arts do this through competitions, structured rank promotions, and demonstrations. These many testing opportunities can also provide some great life memories.

My 1983 Black Belt Test at Jim Mitchell's School in El Cajon, California
Front: L-R: Barry Barker (Me), Ron Jiminez, Margaret Colfer, Derek Jones,
Reverend Mike; Back L-R: Tim Mullins, Jim Mitchell, Ed Parker, Rick Hughes,
Parker Linekin, Darby Darrow, Crane Ponder

The importance of having an advancement and recognition system for students is immeasurable to their motivation, goal-setting, and long-term attendance. Below is a summary of the Belt Ranking System I use at my school as a reference.

Even though Belt Rank Advancement is laid out starting at the bottom then moving to the top, it is less a straight line up like an elevator and more a circular process like a wheel as new levels of mastery are developed followed by new learning and developmental challenges.

Contained are descriptive notes along with a comparison to various college degree levels, and how Ed Parker (EP) titled the various Black Belt levels. The time frames are my standards and represent the fastest way based upon available testing and time in rank.

Note: Black Belts can promote up to the rank below what they are wearing, provided they have authorization from their instructor, association, or organization.

<u>Pre-Black Belt training</u>
Beginning Ranks: White-Yellow-Orange
Intermediate Ranks: Purple-Blue-Green
Advanced Ranks: Red-Any Brown

<u>Black Belt 1st Degree - Associates Degree - Junior Instructor (EP)</u>
An adult at my school takes 3-5 years of curriculum training to reach 1st Degree Black Belt and is required to write and present a Black Belt Thesis. The Associates Degree reference is reflected in the 2-3 classes per week attended by most students or about 3-6 hours of class time weekly.

<u>Black Belt 2nd Degree – Bachelor's Degree - Associate Instructor Rank (EP)</u>
I require a 2-year minimum before my 1st Degree students are eligible for this rank, which also has curriculum and a thesis or project requirement (5-8 years total).

<u>Black Belt 3rd Degree – Master's Degree - Instructor Rank (EP)</u>
I require a 3-year minimum before my 2nd Degree students are eligible for this rank, which also has curriculum and a thesis or project requirement (8-11 years total).

<u>Black Belt 4th Degree - PhD - Senior Instructor Rank (EP)</u>
I require a 4-year minimum before my 3rd Degree students are eligible for this rank (12-15 years total). Since Kenpo trains in street defense I require this rank show additional mastery of our systems weapon and multiple opponent curriculum (Form 6 & Mass Attacks specifically). They are also required to do a project presentation.

<u>Black Belt 5th Degree - Associate Professor Rank (EP)</u>
Starting with this belt rank level a practitioner is promoted due to their training, contribution to martial arts, and their own lobbying efforts, or by recommendation from their instructor. I require a 5-year minimum before my 4th Degree students are eligible for this rank (15-20 years total).

Belt ranks from here forward are for the lifetime martial artist who continues to participate and contribute to the arts in a capacity that suits their expertise, specialty, or interest. I require a minimum of 5-years between subsequent ranks and would expect this level of expert martial artist to be active somewhere in the martial arts world learning, growing, and contributing in some way.

When eligible they are expected to present this experience and growth in the form of a project and present it to a board of their peers and seniors. They have earned the right at this point to physically test in a way of their choosing, or not at all.

<u>Black Belt 6th Degree - Professor Rank (EP)</u>
This represents about 20-25 years active in the martial arts

Black Belt 7th Degree - Senior Professor Rank (EP)
This represents about 25-30 years active in the martial arts

Black Belt 8th Degree - Associate Master of the Arts (AMA) Rank (EP)
This represents about 30-35 years active in the martial arts

Black Belt 9th Degree - Master of the Arts (MA) (EP)
This represents about 35-40 years active in the martial arts

Black Belt 10th Degree - Grand Master of the Arts (GMA) (EP)
This represents a lifetime of study (40 years plus), contribution, and growth. Peers and senior practitioners in the martial arts community would generally, if not publicly recognize this rank. Traditionally there is only one of these in each system, or in modern times, each organization.

Since martial arts ranking is unregulated the integrity of a Black Belt Degree or Rank is self-imposed making for a wide range of standards. For me, my 5-year minimum time in rank often goes by very fast as the lifetime martial artist is in no hurry. A line that is funny, when heard in context from a demo skit we have used for years at my school, aka "Boot to the Head," says it all with the phrase that "time has no meaning; to a true student a year is as a day."

For myself, to honor my time in rank I personally strive to do a personal growth project worthy of that time. Towards this end I have run a full-time school for over 30 years as of this writing, turning out over 65 Black Belts, produced 15 videos, with a Master's Degree in Chinese Medicine and a Licensed Acupuncturist (L.Ac.).

Becoming an author with this 3-book series on the Mind-Body-Spirit of martial arts is my 9th Degree project. I intend for my eventual 10th Degree project to bring me full circle as the mastery of one becomes the start of another

CEREMONY & RITUAL

This is the process by which people are recognized and their accomplishments acknowledged. It is something that takes place after many life accomplishments like graduations, sporting events, and in martial arts with belt rank advancement where the opportunity exists to tap into the power of *Ceremony & Ritual.*

When students are promoted after months, or sometimes years, of challenging work they deserve this recognition and the chance to reflect upon, appreciate, and be recognized for their achievement. The Belt Test Ceremony I have evolved is described below as a sample. It is designed to recognize a student for their efforts, reinforce good life habits, and provide ongoing wisdom to contemplate for future reference.

At the end of a test, students sit with their eyes closed relaxing after a difficult yet completed task. If successful in passing, their new folded belt is placed parallel in front of them where they see it for the first time when they are asked to open their eyes. This begins the ceremony.

They are congratulated on their efforts then asked to go onto their knees, remove their old belts and fold it three times (like the new belt). Place the old belt above the left corner of the new belt forming the letter "L" that represents the "Learning" taking place during our lives and that a love of learning should be with us all.

The observation is made that the belt to their left is the *Past,* and we should honor the past. The new belt in front is the *Present,* and we are to appreciate the present. The open space to the right represents the *Future,* where we maintain hope while striving towards a positive future and growth.

They are then asked to grab the old belt, the past, with their left hand and put it behind them and to "let go of the past" because even though we honor the past we must let it go to see the present more clearly and the larger future once it is removed.

They are then instructed to place their hands on the two edges of their new belt and place their forehead in the middle to show respect for their new rank and initiate that belt with sweat from their test as without sweat there is no worthy accomplishment. They then sit up on their knees holding their new belt in both hands and told that martial arts are about the development of the mind, body, and spirit.

They are instructed to place the new still-folded belt against their foreheads where the mind, mental focus, and intelligence is located and developed. Then against their stomachs under their navel, as this is the center of the body where power and balance is located. Then against their chest or heart where the spirit resides, as this is where determination and drive come from. Then on the ground in front placing their forehead on that belt again to show additional respect for that newly earned and initiated belt.

They then sit up, tie on their new belt and stand where they are bowed out from their test and congratulated by the test board, fellow students, family, and friends.

The attainment of rank through the various levels depends on an individual student's goals, effort, and commitment, with talent a helpful component but one that is not mandatory. Here is the belt ranking structure used at my school.

BELT RANKING STRUCTURE AT POWAY KENPO KARATE

Beginning Ranks
White – Yellow – Orange

Intermediate Ranks
Purple – Blue – Green

Advanced Ranks
Red – Any Brown

Experts Ranks
1st – 2nd – 3rd Degree Black Belt

Senior Experts Ranks
4th – 5th – 6th Degree Black Belt

Masters Ranks
7th – 8th – 9th Degree Black Belt

Grandmasters Rank
10th Degree Black Belt

"WHAT'S UR SHTYLE?"
Chapter III

Many or possibly most martial artists have heard the question at some point over the years as to "What style of martial arts do you study?" This was famously said in the movie *Enter the Dragon* in the boat scene when South African bully Parsons asks Bruce Lee "What's ur Shtyle?" to which Bruce replies "My Style? It is the art of fighting without fighting."

It's a must-see movie for martial arts enthusiasts but suffice to say that this up-front knowledge of someone's style can give insight to an educated practitioner. It can reveal many factors about a person's fighting skill, including type of movement, offensive and defensive strengths, weaknesses, strategies, and emphasis.

This chapter contains a group of articles covering this and other related questions that have been asked of me over my years in martial arts. Subjects covered are the comparisons of a *System, Style, or Art*, the famous *Secrets of the Martial Arts*, the controversial *Religion or Martial Art* topic, and whether we practice a *Sport Art or Street Art*.

There is also a whole section on Kenpo as this is my base art and what I have taught for most of my life. That section includes articles on *"What is Kenpo?"* the spelling controversy of *Kenpo vs Kempo, Characteristics of Kenpo* movement, and two articles that cover history, one on the big picture *History of American Kenpo* and the other on my own *American Kenpo Alliance History* and story.

SYSTEM, STYLE, or ART?

As mentioned, it is common to hear the question "What's your Style?" and martial arts people will often follow the style question with "what system do you study" or perhaps "who is your instructor." A question not often asked is "what's your art?" maybe because, semantics aside, it is often confused with style.

Remember the subject is called martial arts, not martial style. Martial because it is the mind and body's effort to study warfare, fighting, and how to be efficiently violent through a *System*, with *Style* how an individual applies their body to that effort and *Art* the ultimate self-development and expression of the human spirit this produces. These then are the Mind, Body, and Spirit of applied movement.

System

A system is a way of organizing the *Ideas, Theories, Concepts,* and *Principles* needed to accomplish an objective. This is the *Mind* of martial arts that is the component index of basics, techniques, movement exercises and training methods contained within a type of fighting that many may refer to as a "style."

The objective in a system like Kenpo for example is to develop street self-defense skill, or what we sometimes call "sophisticated dirty fighting." The four components practiced too develop this are Basics, Sets & Forms, Sport Fighting, and Self-Defense Techniques (see *Body*). This along with an understanding of human kinetic movement, body anatomy, and physiology are needed for the efficient application of this skill.

Style

The distinguishing factor regarding style is how a practitioner moves and what he personally emphasizes based upon what he was taught, and even its origins. This is the *Body* of martial arts, with diverse cultures emphasizing various fighting methods at various times throughout history, but with the individual applying their own body to the activity.

The word "style" is itself a bit of a misnomer because its essence is one person's trained interpretation and perhaps artistic expression of a system or method. Boxer's box, a Kickboxer kicks and boxes, Wrestler's grapple, Jiu Jitsu practitioners add submission techniques, MMA fighters strike and grapple, and Kenpo people train in street defense. The style is set in motion by the system or method and then interpreted to become a practitioner's unique personal style.

This can be based on body type, temperament, environment, and perhaps even clothing, etc. Some movement styles become more famous than others based upon the success of individual practitioners and training methods that have been handed down over generations of practitioners. This can allow for levels and layers of sophistication to be developed, or for obsolescence to engrain itself.

Some ancient styles copied the movement of animals; others emphasized kicking; some used wide low stances for stability on unstable terrain; others utilized large athletic movements; some preferred striking while others focused on grappling.

These are empty-handed examples but all of the ancient styles, before gun powder weaponry, also practiced with external weapons such as swords, knives, spears, bow and arrow, throwing weapons, and sticks of various lengths. It's a fascinating subject worthy of research for those so inclined.

Styles can be interesting and of course in a fight it can be useful to recognize someone's style as this can guide a knowledgeable practitioner to avoid strengths and take advantage of weaknesses. With that said much of what someone knows and understands could be hidden within their personal movement style as many people, in modern times especially, cross train in multiple styles.

So what style is best? The simple answer is none and all! People do martial arts for different reasons in various cultures at different times to meet different goals, interests, and abilities. The goals of a style can range from increasing one's health to surviving in a violent place and time, or both. Some have a small number of direct killing techniques for use in war where others teach more complete movement methods and uses.

Choices are also affected by culture, historical context, environment, a desire for personal expression, individual strengths, and personal limitations, or the capability of adversaries. They run the full spectrum of age, gender, body type, and athleticism with new styles created by someone to emphasize their preferences, or to fit an environment.

How people have chosen to fight and defend themselves is influenced by these factors and more, so when a style is placed in another culture and context it may have different strengths and weaknesses as compared to what else is being practiced. These are the factors that influence an individual when choosing a style.

Art

This is the personal artistic expression of how an individual applies or demonstrates their movement style and chosen system. This is the *Spirit* expressing itself through martial movement, with the traditional martial art method bringing with it character development benefits as discussed previously. This then helps develop emotional and intellectual maturity allowing for a more complete expression by the individual.

This artistic expression often comes after years of studying a system that evolves into a personal style of movement rooted in that training. It is eventually internalized where it can be released by the practitioner in a free flow of educated artistic expression from their heart and soul.

—

This spirit is rooted in themselves genetically and from their life experiences of which their martial art is a part. At this stage a practitioner's own unique personal dynamics influence this artistic expression as their own style within the system or systems practiced.

The release of this spiritual artistic energy whether practicing, performing, competing, or using these skills for self-defense allows for one's own personal style to evolve, grow, and develop. This is "the glow" made famous in the martial arts spoof "The Last Dragon" or what is referred to in sport vernacular as being "in the zone."

This is when Mind, Body, and Spirit come together in a focused, natural, yet trained way without ego or additional mental interference. It takes years of dedicated effort to master a system and own it as a personal style, and of course we never stop learning and developing as all of this is on a relative continuum with others. The reward however can be incredible and fulfilling on many levels.

A *System* therefore contains everything that can be used to address a martial arts goal, *Style* emphasizes a practitioner's way and emphasis of movement within that system or group of systems, and *Art* is the expression of how the spirit is moved by the experience of these skills.

My answer these days to the question of "what's your style?" is that I study the Ed Parker American Kenpo *System*, my *Style* is my own, and my *Art* is Kenpo Karate/Jiu Jitsu as I evolve it to be in my daily life.

SECRETS OF THE MARTIAL ARTS

As mentioned previously a knowledgeable practitioner can adjust what they do to counter the movement methods and strategies of another style they are familiar with. This reality prompted the need to keep system and style information secret to help avoid this.

Warriors in ancient times would try to keep the "secrets" of their styles mostly unknown while trying to create some illusion and intimidating mystery surrounding what they know and how they train. In modern times fighting contains no real secrets and nothing can or will replace training, learning skill, and gaining insight from a competent teacher, along with talent, genetics, fighting spirit, and determination.

It is true that people re-invent or rediscover things on their own but adaptive people have always searched the universe of ideas to find what works in their time, culture, and environment. Much and possibly most of these discoveries have been documented and stored within martial art systems in separate cultures over the millennium.

This should not be interpreted to mean that there are not levels of knowledge and skill among individual practitioners; or that some don't know more than others; or that people preparing to sport or street fight don't hide their intentions, feint their knowledge, study an adversary; or how one strategy can counter another. Individual dynamics and situations aside my point is the information is available.

The reality is we don't know what we don't know until we know it. Facing this fact makes it possible to search, learn, and discover things that are new to us over our entire lives. Any secret information or discovery not being shared will die with the person carrying it. This type of secret is not only selfish it is mostly useless as someone will re-discover it at some point and then share it with the world. An old Chinese Proverb says it best "if you give it you keep it, if you keep it you lose it."

The places where secret information does still apply is the military and law enforcement where misinformation is let out to confuse and secrets are guarded to keep a potential enemy from knowing technology, tactics, and strategies. Of course, spies still try and often get this information through various means to neutralize or overcome a disadvantage.

This idea of hiding secrets may still be possible in the military but for empty-handed martial arts practitioners in modern times this is virtually impossible (key word virtually). The communication age has made it possible to at least see another styles movement, tactics, and strategies wherever they are being practiced in the world.

Secret knowledge myths do persist individually, and sometimes on a large scale, as a big part of war and fighting is the psychological battle to make an adversary, or potential adversary, believe you know something they don't, or won't be prepared to defend if it were used. The psychology of fighting is supremely important and may even be the most important part.

If someone believes you can touch them in some secret way that will paralyze or kill him or her it can affect the outcome regardless of the reality. If the reputation of a certain art, style, type of person, culture, or individual practitioner puts doubt in your mind then the battle is already partially, if not totally lost.

Any adversary of course needs to be respected, prepared for, and may know something you don't, but psychology and confidence aside there is no secret martial art move or information that cannot be obtained by anyone motivated to obtain it, and everything can be countered.

Even though the heart organ can be damaged with precise striking the practicality of the 5-point palm exploding heart technique (Kill Bill 2) does not exist, and nobody can stop you with the power of his or her "Qi force field," unless you allow it. Voodoo works only on those who believe in it.

The history of warfare and fighting is full of invincible warriors who were defeated by much less skilled or formidable foes. Learn, train, be humble and respectful of all but don't be intimidated or psyched out by unfounded fantasies of super human powers.

Fighting is a very real three-dimensional activity with many variables. It can be sophisticated or mundanely simple but the psychology of secret information beyond that is the mind accepting superstitions that should be avoided.

RELIGION or MARTIAL ART

The question of a relationship between religion and martial arts comes up from time to time. Some worry that by studying martial arts they are prescribing to a religious belief. It's true that many religious people practice martial arts and many martial artists are religious people. The two however are not necessarily related or mutually inclusive of the other.

The word "martial" refers to warriors and warring so martial arts is the study of, or the art of fighting. Religion is the study of the soul and faith in a Supreme Being, God, Deity, or Way of Life.

It is also true that most warriors have strong faith as their experiences have taught them human life is fragile and can be taken at any moment. They respect the power of God as an intangible force that gives them faith and comfort through the ultimate in tough times.

Some confusion comes from the fact that many popular martial arts had their roots in Asian monasteries. The biggest martial arts renaissance began in 5th Century C.E. China at a Buddhist monastery called Shaolin.

Monks living at the Shaolin Temple became exposed to a type of martial art exercise from a Tibetan Buddhist Monk from India named Tamo (DaMo, Bodhidharma). The history and legend behind Tamo is worth researching, but his efforts began the development of Shaolin martial arts.

Over the centuries these monks evolved and developed into a highly skilled martial arts sect. They developed martial arts systems based upon the movements of animals with fighting philosophies influenced by their religion in that their skill was for health and self-defense purposes.

These monks became legendary as they travelled throughout Asia bringing with them martial and healing arts. This became the foundation for many *External* martial art styles practiced throughout the world today.

Another martial arts renaissance began in China around the 14th Century C.E. by Taoists (Daoist) from Wudang (Wutang) Mountain temples. Priests developed *Internal* martial art styles with emphasis on meditative movement with breath and study of herbal concoctions (Taoist Alchemy).

In both cases training in martial arts was part of these Buddhist and Taoist Monks daily life experience, along with chores, philosophy, prayer, meditation, and healing arts. These elements contributed to making them legendary and respected warriors but with fighting skill to be used only if forced to protect themselves or others who were unable.

Through diligent training monks from both sects were able to progress and pass forward higher and higher levels of martial arts knowledge over time. The innovative fighting methods, training techniques, and meditation exercises practiced by them became the foundation for most of the organized martial arts done in the world today.

Shaolin monks especially earned a reputation as very skilled fighter's but, being peaceful religious people, they were still vulnerable. Unlike Wudang, the Shaolin Temple was destroyed several times over hundreds of years causing surviving monks to scatter throughout China and Asia, including Korea, Japan, and Okinawa, taking their martial arts with them.

These monks had only their religion, knowledge of healing arts, and martial arts skill to survive in lands foreign to them. They no doubt came across people who did not buy into their religious philosophy, wanted to rob them, or test their skill.

These skilled and influential Shaolin monks were able to gain respect and acceptance throughout the Asian world. This is a testament to them and the training they received, and no doubt contributed to the popularity of Shaolin based martial arts in modern times.

Many styles trace their roots to this source such as the Korean art Tang Soo Do was named in tribute literally meaning "China Hand Way." Okinawa Te (evolving later to Kara Te) was also strongly influenced by these monks and eventually influenced Japanese martial arts. Shaolin fighting arts mixing with local indigenous fighting methods are part of martial arts historical evolution.

Even though Shaolin monks were religious Buddhists and Wudang Priests religious Taoists their religious doctrines do not discuss fighting methodology and religion is not part of their fighting technique.

The common thread is these were peaceful people who trained for self-preservation. Their knowledge and skill were not intended to be used for sport, personal or financial gain, land, or power. Religious beliefs did however influence their philosophical approach to fighting and combat becoming treatises on "contending" or "not contending," and "moral dilemmas."

Fighting on the other hand happens after most philosophical choices have been made. Religious and non-religious people fight to protect themselves but religion in and of itself does not attach itself to any particular fighting method, but perhaps more of a philosophy about fighting.

Religions true role is in preaching the peace and saving souls while giving internal strength and moral guidance. It is true that many wars have been fought in the name of religion, but those are motivated by men in the name of religion or who use religion for a personal agenda. None of this is a reflection on the teachings or purpose of religion at its highest calling.

SPORT ART or STREET ART

Another of the most often asked question of martial arts instructors, after "what's ur shtyle," would have to be "what is the difference between your style or art and someone else's?"

There are different ways to answer this question. One explanation distinguishes striking arts from grappling arts but the one I am fond of are the differences between sport arts and street arts, since many of these encompass both striking and grappling.

The quick explanation is that sport arts "train to fight" where the intention and hope for street arts is to "train not to fight." Ed Parker formulated what he called "Preparatory Considerations" or "Rules of Combat" of which the first two help define the major differences. Those are *Acceptance* and *Environment*.

Acceptance is a known factor in a sport fight as two opponents prepare and train to fight each other within the rules of the sport. Environment is also known as both show up at the same place and time with the intention of fighting in a ring, a cage, or on a mat.

Acceptance in the street context can be less clear, yet potentially more critical. A street savvy opponent or criminal will often try to disguise their intentions to gain an advantage, and then suddenly attack.

Environment is also unknown in the street and must be instantly assessed to help determine how to avoid hazards and use that environment to our advantage.

Other factors in sport fighting styles like Boxing, Kickboxing, Wrestling, Sport Karate, Sport Jiu Jitsu, Tae Kwon Do, Judo, MMA, etc. is they are all "fair fights" with rules. One unarmed opponent is matched against another unarmed opponent by gender, weight, experience, etc.

In a sport fight the match, bout, and even practice sessions start with one opponent in front of another standing or in a set down position. Both get an equal opportunity to act against a voluntarily positioned opponent willing to respond within the rules of that fighting sport. The fight starts from there but only when they, an instructor, or a referee says to begin.

In a competitive sport fight there is the presumption of sportsmanship with a referee and judges present to assure fair play, settle disputes, try and limit injuries, and determine a winner if both are still fighting when the time runs out. Medical personnel are also usually nearby to treat any injuries. Awards are given and some even receive monetary rewards.

A street confrontation has no such matching or empty-handed 1-on-1 limitations. The street arts can be divided into the three major categories of civilian self-defense taught privately or at commercial schools, law enforcement, and military arts that are taught to professionals in those jobs.

All require moral, legal and practical considerations for determining the level and type of response in a different situation. There are also other variables to consider as it is an unfair fight not matched by size, gender, quantity of attackers, external weapons, etc.

In law enforcement the emphasis is on detaining and controlling a criminal, where the emphasis in military arts is on killing the enemy. In a civilian self-defense "art" the goal is to avoid fighting but still have the skill to respond physically to an unavoidable confrontation.

A street martial arts system is complete when it contains ample information to transcend the different uses. Kenpo, for example, is this type of system in that it can be taught commercially to the general public for self-defense, exercise and personal development, but with a different focus also to law enforcement and the military.

An instructor would determine his or her personal emphasis and student make up to determine what type of training to focus on (e.g. lots of kids and "regular folks" vs. more law enforcement or military students).

Law enforcement requires a lot of controlling techniques so arts like Jiu Jitsu are especially suited to what is commonly needed. Military arts like Krav Maga or Systema need to be modified and regulated for civilian use due to the moral and legal considerations of our litigious world.

In either case attackers involved in a street confrontation are not following any rules and may hide their intentions until they attack. That could occur in any environment from crowded to remote and everything in between. It can come from any direction by one or more than one person with or without weapons. They can be trying to grab, hold, punch, kick, or grapple. The variables are endless in this regard.

There are definite relative strengths and weaknesses in sport and street martial arts styles whether in competition, for civilian self-defense, law enforcement, or military use.

An advantage for sport art training is that a practitioner gets lots of hands on fighting experience against other trained fighters. This also helps limit injuries and allows for more fighting practice over longer periods of time making for a level of experience that is much more difficult for a street fighter to attain without major injury, disability, or death.

Sport fighters also develop a high-level of conditioning, mental toughness, and maturity with this fighting experience. This teaches lessons in how to relax, conserve energy, and think while fighting; all while remaining calm and not panicking in a stressful situation.

The weakness of sport arts is that each practice at ranges and angles allowed in that fighting game. A Boxer stands in front and punches but does not wrestle. A Wrestler grapples but doesn't punch, strike, or kick. An MMA fighter who does both is still not allowed to poke the eyes, attack the groin, grab a finger digit, or have his friends help.

Environment is another factor that can affect sport fighters in a street fight. A Kickboxer would be limited if he got into a fight in a swimming pool, a Boxer may have trouble in a crowded nightclub, a Grappler could have difficulty on asphalt or against more than one opponent.

All would have limited tools to effectively deal with an armed attacker or someone who is much larger; especially if that larger person is skilled. This is the reason weight divisions exist in sport arts.

The strength of street arts is the practice at every range and angle of fighting against one or multiple opponents with and without external weapons. Practice includes using all available natural weapons to any available target including the eyes and other vital areas. This knowledge can help equalize an opponent's other advantages like size or numbers.

The weakness of street arts is that eye pokes and attacking vital areas cannot be practiced with the veracity and commitment needed for actual use. Attacks to eyes, groin, throat, joints, and other vital targets must be practiced with control or nobody would survive a training session.

This can lead to complacency on the part of the person practicing the movement, and the person feeding the attack. Since nobody is really getting injured attackers may not attack or react with the sense of realism for legitimate live application adjustments to be made.

This can lead the street stylist into a false sense of security, believing they have an ability to defend an attack or use a move they have never really applied or felt. This is something the street stylist must guard against.

My belief is that a martial arts practitioner should do both sport and street training. This combination can provide the overall tools, awareness, and experience necessary while providing a competitive outlet for any fighting aggression. It is also a way to stay or become humble, which is the best way to avoid street confrontations while having real confidence to carry us peacefully through life.

WHAT IS KENPO KARATE?

KEN (Fist) PO (Law)

KARA (Empty) TE (Hand)

The Law of the Fist and the Empty Hand

Kenpo is a hybrid martial art style evolving in post WWII Hawaii as a combination of primarily Japanese and Chinese martial arts, but with Polynesian martial arts and other types of fighting also having an influence. This combining of information, fighting philosophy, and traditions has led Kenpo movement to be widely interpreted with a spectrum of movement ranging from very linear and hard to very flowing and soft, and everything in between.

Historical evolution aside, Kenpo Karate is mostly taught as a progressive street / self-defense martial arts system that utilizes linear and circular movements that rapidly connect through spherical orbits and are strategically applied to incapacitate an opponent(s). Kenpo practitioners train at every range and angle of fighting while studying the laws of applied motion.

The mindset of the Kenpo system is to methodically account and train for major attack possibilities with an expectation of unknown variables or "what ifs." This is done with scientific precision and anatomical awareness that allows the practitioner to apply what works best for them based upon the situation, their experience, and personal skill level.

Kenpo practitioners train in pre-arranged self-defense techniques that give way to free form self-defense movements. These self-defense combinations teach how to use these concepts and principles of applied motion against vital targets. This repetition develops muscle memory and gives insight into the most appropriate response needed as determined by the attack and the situation.

With that said, the goal of a civilian martial arts system, as Kenpo is often taught, is to not fight. Using dangerous skills against another person is not sought for moral, legal, and personal safety reasons.

The ultimate training goal of the Kenpo practitioner however is to have the ability and capability to defend against the mass or multiple opponent attack. Most fighting styles focus on one person, with Kenpo also spending a good amount of time on one person, but at the core of Kenpo is how the movements can connect indefinitely onto one or more than one person.

The original American Kenpo System, along with evolved versions like what I teach, offer individual and multiple opponent self-defense techniques and movement forms where these are indexed and linked together against multiple attackers.

Forms are a good place to see this within a theme. In Kenpo Form 3 for example, all the attacks grab, hug, or hold; Form 4 attacks all punch, strike and kick; Form 5 indexes takedowns; and Form 6 defends against knives, clubs, and guns.

These intricate and sophisticated patterns are practiced in the air and can also be done with attackers. Attack scenarios are practiced by theme with attacks from different ranges and angles by one individual, or more than one alternating or attacking simultaneously. To defend oneself in this multiple opponent situation requires attackers to go down quickly and not get up for at least a while.

Rapid-fire Kenpo techniques use formulated combinations that set up a fights endpoint, often with vital target striking (see *Pressure Point* chapter in the *Body*). Kenpo also practices a type of vital target attack I like to call the "nuclear weapons of Kenpo." These "nukes" are a last resort option we hope to never use and are reserved for the worst-case scenario. This knowledge can provide confidence and control that can deflect and deter the need for its use.

They are Eye attacks for example are part of advanced Kenpo training. Kenpo is unmatched when it comes to attacking the eyes. These are not taught to beginners where it could be dangerous to pass this knowledge on due to age, temperament, attitude, maturity, or control to safely practice. This knowledge and skill is to be kept in reserve for emergency use only, so it must be earned.

There are four methods of applying the fingers as weapons to the eyes. These are practiced primarily in the Kenpo *Finger Sets* and offered, usually as "hidden moves," within many and possibly most of the Kenpo self-defense techniques. The Basics chapter in my *Body* book covers this in detail but the four categories for using the fingers as weapons are poke, slice, whip, and claw.

These methods are used extensively in advanced Kenpo technique practice as the eyes are one of the easiest targets to attack. This along with the neck region, groin, and ears are great equalizers to size, strength, athleticism, energy, ferocity, and determination. Having this knowledge makes these an excellent emergency backup available to the Kenpo practitioner.

Simply stated, Kenpo is the art of "dirty fighting" but also is a complete and thorough martial art system, with its commercial emphasis on civilian self-defense. When presented in the traditional format it can also be used to develop discipline, confidence, and other positive character attributes.

KENPO OR KEMPO?

A rule of the Japanese dialect, as I understand it, is that when a "tongue made" sound, like "N" is combined with a "lip made" sound like "P" the "N" is softened to an "M" sound. This is most likely where the confusion surrounding the spelling originates, as the written Japanese Kanji does not look like any of the Western Latin letters used to spell it.

My former instructor, Jim Mitchell, had told me a version of this phonetic vs. linguistic spelling story but I had a chance to ask the man himself at one point. One day in 1989 Mr. Parker called me regarding some tournament applications I had sent for the International Karate Championships that year. I took the opportunity to ask him to explain to me the differences in the spelling between "Kenpo" and "Kempo."

He told me pretty much the same story I had heard earlier adding that he had verified it through two Japanese linguists. This, along with my own research confirmed it more clearly in my mind.

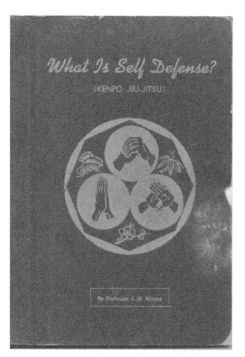

After Mr. Parker told me that story I was feeling a little above all those ignorant "mis-spellers" of our art. I guess Mr. Parker sensed my arrogance because he repeated to me a famous quote attributed to him, *"remember Barry when pure knuckles meet pure flesh, that's pure karate and it doesn't matter how you spell it."* Needless to say, I was appropriately humbled and said, "yes sir."

A few years later, after Mr. Parker had passed away, I came across a copy of James Mitoses book from 1947 called "What is Self-Defense (Kenpo Jiu Jitsu)." In that book there are several testimonial letters from friends, students, and local government people acclaiming the merits of his book. The letters are divided into two groups from two different years (see samples).

In the first group of letters from 1947 the art is always spelled KEMPO.
In the second group of letters from 1953 the art is always spelled KENPO.

It appears from these letters that at some point between 1947 and 1953 James Mitose changed his spelling from Kempo to Kenpo.

---

over your new book, "What is S i. I am sure our borrowers will find
Kempo Jiu-jitsu", and find it rt of Kenpo jiu-jitsu most interesting
and educational on the art of l addition to our library collection.

William Chow is in many of the pictures contained in that book as well,
but he was not training with Mitose in 1953. This might explain why Chow
never used the updated spelling, or he determined the application of
technique did not require those spelling particulars and left it alone.

Since everyone involved is now deceased we can only evaluate the history,
listen to everyone's version, including anecdotes, and reach our own
conclusions. I have concluded that the Kenpo spelling controversy must
have started with English speaking students phonetically translating the
name as they heard it from their Japanese instructor James Mitose. This
carried over to William Chow who learned his Kenpo from Mitose.

Mitoses early lineage students spell it "Kempo" while later one's spell it
"Kenpo." Professor Chow's lineage spells it either "Kempo" or "Kenpo"
depending on preference (e.g. Kaju<u>ken</u>bo, American <u>Ken</u>po, Kara-Ho
<u>Kem</u>po, etc.).

At this point neither the phonetic or linguistic spelling groups need to nor
would they change how they spell their arts. It is one of those things we
accept then move on to training and perhaps more important discussions.

CHARACTERISTICS OF KENPO

A style of martial arts tends to develop characteristics based on the type of techniques favored, or rules as in sport fighting, and is influenced by the personal dynamics of a teacher or system founder. This can be seen in the styles posture as Wrestlers stand differently than Boxers for example.

Kenpo has such a group of characteristics that help define its style and type of movement. These and other uniform movement characteristics can also be seen in other styles but collectively make Kenpo unique.

Explosiveness
Kenpo begins from total calmness and relaxation, then explodes to maximum speed, power, and energy in a heartbeat. This Kenpo method of fighting is sometimes described as "like dynamite, it does not gradually explode." The Kenpo stylist does not gradually attain full fighting energy but is calm, then BOOM!!!, goes off like a bomb with an explosion of continuous movement that does not stop until the altercation has ended.

Kenpo Flow – Sequential Flow – Compounded Energy
A continuous flow of integrated, bilateral, and gaseous spherical motion strategically applied through linear and circular paths for maximum protection with the chosen possibility of maximum destruction, devastation, and/or annihilation.

Every weapon connects to another weapon continuously in a logical efficient movement progression that builds upon previous moves and target reactions until we choose to stop, and what my friend Master Rick Hughes calls "putting a tomato in a blender." See *Sequential Flow, Compounded Energy* and *Muscle Pre-Load* in the *Mind*.

Rooted
This term is often used in Tai Chi and there denotes visualizing roots growing from the bottoms of the feet. This makes for a strong mental connection with the ground that becomes a firm and real physical one. Striking power especially comes from this earth's leverage transferred through the feet and legs making this feet-rooting important for stability and power.

This foot to ground rooting can be akin to a fire hydrant. It is supremely stable, and nobody attacks a fire hydrant without paying a price. This is one mental image Kenpo practitioners can have of themselves while fighting, rooted like a fire hydrant, but still able to move.

Head Level Movement
This has to do with moving through a bent knee position while maintaining an erect posture and is observed as the head moving at the same level. Just as a racecar goes fastest on a flat drag strip with no hills or speed bumps we also travel more effectively in this way. Kenpo movement can also appear as though skating on the ground.

This type of movement requires that our feet slide or lightly feel the ground as we move. This allows us to align action and direction, so we are not moving up and down while applying energy on a horizontal plane parallel with the ground.

An additional bonus of this type of movement is that it becomes more difficult for an opponent to pick up changes in our depth. This occurs because the light around us that forms our silhouette does not perceptively change when advancing (or retreating) in this level manner.

Since we are not always on flat terrain our legs must act like shock absorbers that constantly adjust to the ground we are on. Fighting, like any other athletic activity, cannot be done well with straight legs. Moving with slightly bent knees allows us to accelerate, remain mobile, and utilize gravity to leverage our power while maintaining a level head position.

Range Manipulation
Once movement is known, the application of that movement to be effective on an unwilling adversary requires awareness of structure, anatomy, targets, weapons, unbalancing techniques, weight transfer, muscle pre-load knowledge, feel, along with natural and reflexive reactions. This knowledge brings the techniques alive to control and move an opponent by pulling, pushing, hitting, twisting, sweeping, or bumping to orchestrate position change. This is known in Kenpo as "carrying an opponent."

Nuclear Weapons
The **G**reat **E**qualizers: **T**hroat-**G**roin-**E**yes & **E**ars
Kenpo is not only designed to benefit the strong as the weak, outnumbered, and overmatched can take comfort in the practice and knowledge of developing the "Nuclear Option" of Kenpo (See "Nuclear Weapons of Kenpo). **T**he **G**reat **E**qualizers is what I call them in women's self-defense classes. This nuclear option is what can level the playing field in a life and death struggle.

The **T** in "**T**he" relates to the **T**hroat, along with the neck and cervical spine. This area can be struck, grabbed, poked, choked, squeezed, twisted, and even bitten. Since human survival is transmitted through the throat and neck by air, blood, and nerve function the Kenpo practitioner spends a considerable amount of time learning methods to attack and defend this vital weak link on the human body.

The **G** in "**G**reat" relates to the **G**roin, which can be struck, stomped, grabbed and squeezed. When attacking the groin of a man it is important to know the most effective target is the testicles, which is best attacked from underneath and driven up to be crushed against the pubic bone.

Although difficult to attack, as men also know of this vulnerability, Kenpo practitioners become experts at attacking the groin from many angles and positions, and with different weapons. The frontal groin attack has some effectiveness, but this lower abdominal attack is recovered from relatively quickly by a determined adversary so follow ups must be immediate.

The **E** in "**E**qualizers" is for **E**ye and **E**ar attacks.
The **E**yes are attacked in Kenpo from every possible angle using pokes, slices, whips, and claws. These can be done as an initial entry move, be hidden within the flow of action, or be the final blow that assures victory. An eye injury severely limits anyone's ability to function from the vision disruption to the pain and panic that can accompany damage to this area.

The **E**ars are primarily attacked with a slap, clap, or cupping of the hands around the holes of the ears. This technique compresses and pressurizes the eardrum and can dramatically affect a person's equilibrium (balance) and mental focus, while potentially rupturing the eardrum. The result is dizziness and vertigo that provides follow-up vulnerability or gives more escape time.

With "The Great Equalizers" remember "It doesn't take a sledge hammer to kill a fly," so accuracy is important. These are only for use if in severe danger so trust your instincts, but if in doubt consider the saying, "It's better to be tried by twelve than carried by six."

Awareness
The focused presence on a situation from the "Black Dot" and "White Dot" perspective (see the *Mind* and *Body* books) where the mind, body and spirit are fully engaged and able to function effectively.

This "mind of no mind" from Japanese Budo, or the being "in the zone" concept as described in sports is when mental obstacles like ego, wishful thinking, and fear are removed. This leaves an unbiased uncluttered understanding of current reality allowing for a heightened state of consciousness and performance.

Fighting Spirit
Even though a street style like Kenpo trains <u>not</u> to fight when/if the decision and action <u>to</u> fight has been triggered the intensity and drive to win must be relentless. A controlled viciousness appropriate to the situation must be tapped into for this victory to be achieved. This requires an enthusiastic desire to effectively apply the techniques to the effect needed. Holding back is a sure way to lose, even with well-chosen technique.

One of my favorite responses to a fight challenge comes from my friend, Tai Chi Instructor, and Kenpo Master Rey Leal. He tells a story that under one such provocation he looked at the instigator and said, "I <u>don't like</u> to fight" (pause), "I <u>love</u> to fight" (crazy look), prompting the adversary to back down in that instance.

—

HISTORY OF AMERICAN KENPO

The Kenpo Karate described in this book series is commonly referred to as American Kenpo, as SGM Edmund K. Parker termed his unique system that was influenced and continues evolving in the American culture. This martial art has been and continues to be developed to fit the American mind set, methods of learning, and the freethinking questioning spirit we are famous, or perhaps infamous for.

There are numerous books on the history of the martial arts evolving from the Shaolin Temple, so this book will not repeat that whole story. The history contained here begins in Hawaii where his American Kenpo was born. Kenpo is spelled here with an "n" how Mr. Parker wanted it.

Kenpo Karate is a modern, progressive street self-defense art originally taught in Hawaii by James Mitose, who was Japanese but born in Hawaii then raised as a youth in Japan, where he learned his family art of Kosho Ryu Kempo. After spending his youth living in Japan he returned to Hawaii and as a young man was there when Pearl Harbor was bombed in 1941. This must have been a conflicting time for him, but he chose to teach martial arts to the Territorial National Guard.

James Mitose also taught his "Kenpo Jiu Jitsu" (title of his 1947 book) to, among others, William KS (Thunderbolt) Chow in the 1940's. "Professor Chow" as he would become known, combined this knowledge with previous training from his families Kung Fu style learned as a child from his father, Hoon Chow. He combined these with his knowledge and experience as a well-known and feared island street fighter and began teaching other locals who wanted to learn how to fight better.

In those days Hawaii was a melting pot of many Asian cultures, American military personnel, and the islands indigenous people. Japanese, Chinese, Koreans, Okinawans, Filipinos, Americans, and locals were mixing together in the city and neighborhoods.

Rumor, and story, has it there was a lot of real life testing going on in those days on the mean streets of Honolulu. Out of those tough times came some effective martial arts. Professor Chows "Kara-Ho Kempo" became respected as one of the most fierce and effective arts from that era.

Several of Professor Chow's students went on to evolve their own arts or expand and evolve what he had shown them. The Emperado brothers formed "Kajukenbo" for example but undoubtedly his most well-known student was Edmund Kealoa Parker (1931-1990) who went on to form "American Kenpo."

Mr. Parker's training with Professor Chow would prove to be his calling in life. After high school he attended Brigham Young University in Provo Utah. His wife Leilani told me in a 1991 telephone conversation that he earned a Bachelor's Degree in Sociology with a minor in Psychology.

—

While there, he eventually taught self-defense courses, other students, and law enforcement personnel. Through these connections he received a job offer in Los Angeles but after moving the offer fell through, so he decided to open a Kenpo Karate School in Pasadena in 1956 (see Mr. Parkers Books 1 & 2 for this complete history directly from him).

Mr. Parker's school was one of the first commercial martial arts schools open to the general public in the United States, and the first Kenpo School.

Mr. Parker was a great practitioner and teacher but was also an outstanding businessman and entrepreneur. He ran a successful school, formed what would become the largest Kenpo organization in the world (the IKKA), and started what became the largest and most prestigious karate tournament in the country, if not the world, for many years.

The International Karate Championships became the showpiece that launched the careers of many famous martial artists, most notably Bruce Lee and Chuck Norris. Other practitioners also had their lives and careers affected by Mr. Parker, including Joe Lewis, Bill Wallace, Bennie Urquidez, Dan Inosanto, and Jeff Speakman, to name a few.

It would not be an exaggeration to say that Mr. Parker was the seed from which sprang the most influential martial artists of the 20th Century. He is responsible for discovering and displaying the talent that would bring martial arts to the mainstream of American society. He was also the personal bodyguard and a close personal friend of Elvis Presley.

For Kenpo practitioners, Mr. Parker's greatest gifts are the books he wrote for us to study, analyze, reflect, and learn from. His love of motion is obvious when reading any of these books. His analytical and organizational skill provides an incredible amount of insight into the levels of learning and discovery contained within Kenpo technique.

Unfortunately, Mr. Parker passed away before he could complete his video project, but the two videos he did complete show the thoroughness with which he could cover this subject.

When talking with "old-timers" who trained personally with Mr. Parker there is still a very strong sense of loyalty, respect, admiration, and amazement for his abilities, knowledge, and wisdom. He was surely a great man and a martial artist who is greatly missed, especially by those who knew him personally.

AMERICAN KENPO ALLIANCE (AKA) HISTORY

Many of Mr. Parker's students have made martial arts their life's work. Three of those, Brian Adams, Jim Mitchell, and Ernest George Jr., are my foundation in Kenpo. Of course, teaching Kenpo at my school for over 30 years, as of this writing, has given me the opportunity to attain additional insights.

I became fascinated with martial arts as a 10-year-old living in San Diego, California. My fascination with watching Batman and Robin beat up bad guys every week was replaced by my obsession with watching Kato in the Green Hornet beat up bad guys with cool "Karate" moves.

I enjoyed the show so much I even dressed as Kato for Halloween that year. I remember my mom being worried that a car would hit me that night because I was dressed all in black. I didn't of course as I stealthily moved from house to house collecting candy.

My martial arts interest was piqued but the problem was that in 1965 there were no martial art schools around my area that taught kids, so I just imagined and pretended. I was a gymnast, wrestled, and ran track in high school until a senior year restaurant job took me away from sports.

During this time, in the early 1970's, a group of "chop-socky" cheesy kung fu movies became popular. My high school buddy, Pete Beretta, and I would go see them all. When "Enter the Dragon" came out I saw Bruce Lee again and was re-inspired to learn martial arts.

When I graduated from high school in 1973, I enrolled at an Ed Parker's Kenpo Karate School run by Mr. Brian Adams where I trained for approximately 6 months and received my first promotion, under then 1st Degree Black Belt instructor Parker Linekin. I had a girlfriend and a job and decided to attend junior college. Martial arts gave way to those other pursuits.

In college I enrolled in every martial arts course offered and I even took fencing and dance classes. Anything to do with coordinated movement fascinated me as I also took several semesters of Tai Chi at the La Mesa Recreation Center.

I always practiced what I had learned, and I even entered my first karate tournament in 1978. At that tournament I wore my red belt that Parker Linekin had awarded me a few years earlier for attaining my first rank at Brian Adams School.

Little did I know a Red Belt for beginners at my school was considered a Brown Belt everywhere else, so I competed in the Brown/Red Belt division even though technically a Yellow Belt. Needless to mention I didn't win, and the details makes for a good story that I will tell if prompted.

This is when I first saw and met the bigger than life Mr. Parker who had come down from L.A. to watch the tournament and was sitting behind me in the bleachers where we briefly chatted. I was also able to see some incredible local San Diego martial artists compete, some who went on to become local legends.

Three of those, Orned "Chicken" Gabriel, Rey Leal, and Steve "Nasty" Anderson, were highly skilled, spirited, and inspiring martial artists. I had never seen that level of performance and fighting skill in person before, so I was re-motivated to take formal classes.

In 1980, I found an Ed Parker school in El Cajon near my home run by one of Mr. Parker's personal students, Mr. Jim Mitchell. He was a 4th Degree Black Belt at that time and is pictured doing the stance-work in Mr. Parker's Infinite Insights book series, Volume 2. He was a very precise and detailed instructor who emphasized basics, so that worked out well for my foundational early training.

At that time, I worked at Buck Knives in El Cajon, was married with two children, Justin and Alexis. I was finally settled enough to train regularly in what I had wanted to do since I was 10 years old, martial arts, and I became obsessed with Kenpo. My wife at the time used to tell me I would even get up in the middle of the night, while still sleeping, and do forms and techniques.

For my brown belt test, in 1982, we all went to Mr. Parker's school in Pasadena, California. I remember that the floor was lumpy, and my test board included Mr. Parker, Mr. Mitchell, Mr. Frank Trejo, Mr. Ron Chapel, and others whom I don't remember.

It was very stressful and exhausting, but I passed and became a brown belt. We attended an "Advanced Theories Seminar" while there and then returned home.

My 1st Degree Black Belt test was at my home school in 1983, and with Mr. Parker coming down to sit on the test board I prepared extra hard. After passing that test, we took some great pictures, and then we all went out to dinner. I remember Mr. Parker was robust, ordered a big steak, had a big personality and it was an enjoyable experience and a nice memory.

In 1984 Mr. Mitchell had a falling out with Mr. Parker over things beyond my knowledge, or interest. I stayed with Mr. Mitchell because he was my instructor and I had more direct ties to him, and his school was a block from my house. I still had a sense of loyalty to Mr. Parker even though the two of them no longer spoke.

Mr. Mitchell moved away to Oregon, I changed jobs and was going through a divorce, so I needed to stay busy. To train consistently I decided to open my own school, Aaction Kenpo Karate, which was my affiliation to Mr. Mitchell, on October 1, 1984 (also my son Justin's 9th Birthday), in an old 600 sf house on Poway Road in Poway California.

After six months I was able to rent a 900-sf commercial space, also on Poway Road (everything in Poway was on Poway Road then). After nine months I was able to rent a 1,900-sf space in the Lively Center strip mall, again on Poway Road. For the first two years I was in business I had a regular full-time job as a Production Manager at National Pen Corporation and ran my Karate School after work.

Eventually I quit that job and started running my school full time. In 1988 I met a Kenpo Black Belt girl from Texas named Rosie. I talked her into moving to California in 1989 and married her in 1992. She had two children, Josh & Jessica Lara, then 6 and 5 years old who I helped raise and consider my own kids. Rosie and I had our son Jordan in 1993.

Jim Mitchell who lived in Missouri at that time promoted me to 4th Degree in 1990, the same year Mr. Parker died. My school was growing so I moved into a 3000-sf facility in 1991. Shortly after that Mr. Mitchell and I lost our teacher/student connection, so I broke away from his WKKA organization and changed my school name to Poway Kenpo Karate and formed my own association, the American Kenpo Alliance (AKA).

I realized that I still needed an instructor, so I contacted Mrs. Parker at IKKA headquarters looking for a high level IKKA Black Belt who would be close enough for me to train under. She put me in touch with Ernest George Jr. in nearby San Juan Capistrano, California (60 miles away). I contacted Mr. George and we hit it off instantly and I learned from him every time I saw or even spoke with him over the ten years he was my instructor.

Mr. George promoted me to 5th Degree in 1995 and 6th degree in 2000, with my first Black Belt instructor, Master Parker Linekin, able to witness these promotions. My seniors in Kenpo, friends, and former Ed Parker personal students Masters Rick Hughes and Willy Steele promoted me to 7th Degree in 2005. In 2010, Grandmaster Parker Linekin with approval from Great Grandmaster Brian Adams promoted me to 8th Degree.

During this time, I added a sport fighting facility to my business with a Muay Thai gym in 1998, changing that to a Boxing Gym in 2001. I added Brazilian Jiu Jitsu in 2005, then a full MMA gym in 2008.

My facility in Poway California currently offers Kenpo Karate, Boxing, Muay Thai, and Brazilian Jiu Jitsu. I became a Licensed Acupuncturist along the way graduating with a Master's Degree in Oriental Medicine from Pacific College of Oriental Medicine in 2007. I started this three-book project in 2010 to finish by 2015 as my 9th Degree thesis that will hopefully make me worthy of promotion to 9th Degree at some point. To be continued...

FOR ALL MARTIAL ARTISTS
Chapter IV

This chapter covers intangibles that affect our mental and physical health. These affect our spirit, and how we progress and grow in life.

The subject of timeless "Wisdom" whether philosophy, knowledge, or self-discipline can lead to good life habits. This can then lead to the continual attainment of higher levels of knowledge and personal growth.

I believe this is best accomplished with a self-vision for our life that is motivated by a desire to grow, succeed, and not quit. This vision is driven by a controlled yet motivated "Ego" that keeps us putting in the work necessary to gain the knowledge that leads to the understanding to fulfill that vision.

This self-vision is the basis of our life habits from simple things like brushing our teeth to more complex educational goals, career aspirations, relationships, etc. Whatever the vision, or however the unpredictable nature of life causes adjustments to be made, it is our spirit that keeps us moving down our life's path. During this time, we gain skill and life experience, hopefully while enjoying the journey.

In developing our self as martial artists a "Mind-Body-Spirit Connection" evolves. This is where muscle memory (Body) with mental memory and knowledge (Mind) merge and overlap with effort and passion (Spirit). This again is the meaning of the "mind of no mind" phrase from Asian martial arts, the idea of moving without conscious thought, a Zen moment, in the moment, or being "in the zone" as described in sports.

Reaching and hopefully exceeding our personal self-vision is best accomplished with a positive mental attitude where our spirit remains motivated as we go through life, hopefully seeing the glass as half-full.

This also means trying to avoid images and ideas that can poison our mind along with physical toxins that can corrupt our body as we strive to lead a balanced healthy life.

Presuming a martial artist has this self-vision there would be a desire for good physical health through informed "Nutrition" and knowledge of smart "Exercise Basics." This would all be tempered through being "tested" in several ways to fully grow from the effort. This all can lead to a meaningful life that is full of successes and positive memories.

WISDOM

For assorted reasons martial arts has developed a reputation for passing on useful life knowledge, or "wisdom." Listed here are some of my favorites divided into the two categories of "Philosophy" and "Training - Competing - Fighting."

Many of these come from well-known people with a few from lesser known ones, plus some of my own sayings and thoughts from over the years. I have attributed these quotes where I know who is credited as the originator, but some are attributed to the person I heard them from, granted they may have heard them from someone else, etc.

Obviously, it would be impossible to include every great bit of wisdom available as we all come across these and other gems throughout life. Please feel free to take any that you enjoy for your own collection. Also added at the end are a few "Analogies" and "Metaphors" used by martial arts teachers, the "Language of Motion" summary, and some of my favorite martial arts related books are listed.

Philosophy

"He who tries for small advantages never achieves great things."
- Confucius

"He who has seen little marvels at much."
- Confucius

"The ultimate aim of Karate lies not in victory or defeat, but in the perfection of the character of its participants."
- Gichin Funakoshi

"To win one hundred victories in one hundred battles is not the highest skill. To subdue the enemy without fighting is the highest skill."
- Sun Tsu

"Mastering others requires force; Mastering the self requires enlightenment."
- Lao Zi

"If you want to be full, first let yourself become empty."
- Lao Zi

"To know yet to think that one does not know is best. Not to know yet to think that one knows will lead to difficulty."
- Lao Z

"To die but not to perish is to be eternally present."
- Lao Zi

"The sage has no mind of his own, He is good to people who are good. He is also good to people who are not good, because essence is goodness."
    - Lao Zi

"The sages do not consider that making no mistakes is a blessing. They believe, rather, that the great virtue of man lies in his ability to correct his mistakes and continually make a new man of himself."
    - Wang Yang-Ming

"The great man is he who does not lose his child's heart."
    - Mencius

"Fools show annoyance at once, but the prudent overlook insult."
    - The Bible (Proverbs 12:16)

"What's important is to try to develop insights and wisdom rather than mere knowledge, respect someone's character rather than his learning, and nurture men of character rather than mere talents."
    - Inazo Nitobe

"If you give it, you keep it. If you keep it, you lose it."
    - Chinese Proverb

"Give a man a fish, feed him for a day; teach him how to fish, feed him for a lifetime."
    - Maimonides

"Knowledge which stops at what it does not know is the fullest knowledge."
    - Zhuang Zi

"It is better to travel well than to arrive."
    - Buddha

"Noble Eight-Fold Path: Right Understanding, Right Thought, Right Speech, Right Action, Right Livelihood, Right Effort, Right Mindfulness, Right Concentration."
    - Buddha

"The mind is the presence of intention, the eyes are the focus of intention, movement is the action of intention, breath is the flow of intention."
    - Chi Gung principles, author unknown to me

"One man's/person's freedom ends where another man's/person's starts."
    - paraphrased from different sources

"A man wrapped up in himself makes a very small bundle."
    - Benjamin Franklin

"The Four Agreements: 1) Be impeccable with your word; 2) Don't take anything personally; 3) Don't make assumptions; 4) Always do your best."
- Don Miguel Ruiz (thank you Josh)

"Discipline is the bridge between Goals and Accomplishments."
- Jim Rohn

"It is the set of the sails not the direction of the wind that determines which way we will go."
- Jim Rohn

"Be yourself; everyone else is already taken."
- Oscar Wilde

"A pessimist sees the difficulty in every opportunity where an optimist sees the opportunity in every difficulty."
- Winston Churchill

"No one can make you feel inferior without your consent."
- Eleanor Roosevelt

"Great minds discuss ideas, average minds discuss events, small minds discuss people."
- Eleanor Roosevelt

"Learn from the mistakes of others, you can't live long enough to make them all yourself."
- Sam Levenson

"Learn from the past, but don't live there. Plan for the future, but don't live there."
- Spencer Johnson

"Don't cry because it's over, smile because it happened."
- Dr Seuss

"Fear is the thief of dreams."
- Brian Krans

"You must absorb what you have learned before you can learn what you have absorbed."
- Author unknown to me

"Ability is what you're capable of doing. Motivation determines what you do. Attitude determines how well you do it."
- Lou Holtz

"Things turn out best for the people who make the best of the way things turn out."
- John Wooden

"Talent is God given. Be humble. Fame is man-given. Be grateful. Conceit is self-given. Be careful."
  - John Wooden

"When is a man *In* mere understanding? I answer: When a man sees one thing separated from another. And when is a man *Above* understanding? That I can tell you: When a man sees All in All, then a man stands beyond mere understanding."
  - Eckhart Tolle

"This too shall pass."
  - The Bible (Corinthians 10:12)

"Knowledge is bound when one is compelled to tradition. Knowledge is endless when tradition is bound."
  - Ed Parkers Book 1 not attributed

"A wise man can learn more from a foolish question than a fool can learn from a wise answer."
  - Bruce Lee

"Have no way as way; Have no limitation as limitation."
  - Bruce Lee

"Not to understand a man's purpose does not make him confused" & "To not know another man's purpose does not reflect confusion on his part."
  - Master Po (Kung Fu Series)

"Procrastinate tomorrow."
  - Snoopy Cartoon (cartoon note on my bulletin board forever)

"Your Attitude, not your Aptitude, will determine your Altitude."
  - Zig Ziglar (paraphrased sign above my school's entrance for years)

"Wherever shadows fall, light is nearby."
  - A summary of many shadow quotes, author unknown to me

Barry Barker Philosophy Quotes:
"The ultimate in ego is to believe there is no God."

"The atheist cannot believe in God because he has become God."

"God creates, man discovers and rearranges."

"Organization does not form out of chaos without Intention."

"The key to wisdom is in accepting obvious truths."

"Be humble because even though *our* world revolves around us, *the* world does not!" & "Each of us is the center of *our* own Universe but none of us is the center of *the* Universe."

"Principles define the Concepts that prove the Theories which stem from the Ideas."

"A fool ridicules what he does not understand where a wise man looks for value in all things."

"Once you think you know everything, then that is all you will know."

"Success is when you accomplish more than others expected from you but less than you expected from yourself."

"Set yourself up for success."

"Here is my secret to success: Keep showing up!"

"Life is fuller when you have a passion and can share that passion with others."

"Intelligence is being able to recognize that you've learned something."

"In business you are as you are perceived, not as you perceive."

"Age is a number. Don't let it define you."

"Nothing is more annoying than an ignorant person's opinion."

"Accomplishments are, by definition, in the past."

"Our personal life experiences and universal truth discoveries may be new to us, but they are not new to the history of humanity."

"Our lives exist on an overlapping continuum, so nobody's current condition or experience is being felt by or agreed with by all at any given time."

"Only the arrogant and the ignorant think they know more about non-technology related subjects than the collective wisdom of human history."

"Just because we don't understand something, doesn't make it not true."

"In order for war to be just, three things are necessary. First, the authority of the sovereign. Secondly, a just cause. Thirdly, a rightful intention."
- Thomas Aquinas

"Warriors are not what you think of as warriors. The warrior is not someone who fights, because no one has the right to take another life. The warrior, for us, is one who sacrifices himself for the good of others. His task is to take care of the elderly, the defenseless, those who cannot provide for themselves, and above all, the children, the future of humanity."
- Sitting Bull

"If you have no capacity for violence, then you are a healthy productive citizen: a Sheep. If you have a capacity for violence and no empathy for your fellow citizens, then you have defined an aggressive sociopath: a Wolf. But what if you have a capacity for violence, and a deep love for your fellow citizen? Then you are a Sheepdog, a Warrior, someone who is walking the hero's path."
- David Grossman (On Combat), made famous in "American Sniper"

"As iron sharpens iron, so one person sharpens another."
- The Bible (Proverbs 27:17)

"Give me six hours to chop down a tree and I will spend the first four sharpening my axe."
- Abe Lincoln

"He who fails to prepare, prepares to fail."
- Benjamin Franklin (not exact)

"Luck is when Preparation meets Opportunity."
- Roman Philosopher Seneca (paraphrased)

"I am a great believer in luck, and I find the harder I work, the more I have of it." (Paraphrased: The harder I work, the luckier I get)
- Thomas Jefferson

"That which does not kill us makes us stronger."
- Friedrich Nietzsche

"A pint of sweat will save a gallon of blood."
- George S Patton (WWII U.S. General)

"In case of doubt, attack."
- George S Patton (WWII U.S. General)

"Practice doesn't make perfect. Only perfect practice makes perfect."
- Vince Lombardi

"The only place Success comes before Work is in the dictionary."
- Vince Lombardi

"Quitters Never Win and Winners Never Quit."
- Vince Lombardi & Orned "Chicken" Gabriel (Friend/Fight Coach)

"Show me a good loser and I'll show you a loser."
- Vince Lombardi

"It ain't over till it's over."
- Yogi Berra

"In theory there is no difference between theory and practice. In practice there is."
- Yogi Berra

"Quantity has a Quality all its own."
- Russian General (Joseph Stalin)

"He who excels in combat is one who does not let himself be roused."
- Lao Tzu

"Nothing in the world can take the place of Persistence. Talent will not; nothing is more common than unsuccessful men with talent. Genius will not; unrewarded genius is almost a proverb. Education will not; the world is full of educated derelicts. Persistence and determination along are omnipotent. The slogan 'Press On' has solved and always will solve the problems of the human race."
Calvin Coolidge (permanent copy on bulletin board next to my desk)

"Don't watch the clock; do what it does. Keep going."
- Sam Levenson

"Power is created in the mind, rooted in the feet, developed in the legs, directed by the hips, transferred through the torso, focused in the feet or hands and felt in the spirit."
- C.J. Doyle;
* My addition to the previous CJ Doyle quote: **"Power is given Intention through the eyes and Flows with the Breath."**

"It's not the size of the dog in the fight it's the size of the fight in the dog."
- Mark Twain and my mom

"The bigger they are, the harder they fall."
- Joe "The Barbados Demon" Walcott (arguably) and also my mom

"One excuse is as good as another."
- my mom again

"It's better to be tried by 12 than carried by 6."
- Version of cultural slang, author unknown to me

"The key to immortality is first living a life worth remembering."
- Bruce Lee (and a tattoo on my son Jordan's forearm)

"Knowing is not enough, we must apply. Willing is not enough, we must do."
- Bruce Lee

"I fear not the man who has practiced 10,000 kicks once, but the man who has practiced one kick 10,000 times"
- Bruce Lee

"A good fight should be like a small play but played seriously. A good martial artist does not become tense, but ready. Not thinking yet not dreaming, ready for whatever may come. When the opponent expands I contract, when he contracts I expand and when there is an opportunity I do not hit, it hits all by itself."
- Bruce Lee (Enter the Dragon)

"Empty your mind. Be formless. Shapeless. Like Water. You put water into a cup, it becomes the cup. You put water into a bottle, it becomes the bottle. You put water into a teapot, it becomes the teapot. Water can flow, or it can crash. Be water my friend."
- Bruce Lee

"Practicality borders between Simplicity and Complexity."
- Ed Parker

"To hear is to doubt, to see is to be deceived, but to feel is to believe."
- Ed Parker

"When pure knuckles meet pure flesh, that's pure Karate, no matter who executes it or what style is involved." (or as he told me "how you spell it")
- Ed Parker

"To beat action, meet action."
- Ed Parker

"Principles of motion take precedent over Sequences of motion."
- Ed Parker

"Many answers lie in a single move." (with optional follow-up): "but many moves do not necessarily give a single answer."
- Ed Parker

"Guts and conditioning take over where skill and knowledge leave off."
- Ed Parker

—

"If you can't get out of a fight, get into it."
- Ed Parker

"The secret of the martial arts is not to have knowledge of twenty-four things as it is in knowing four things {well}. That is the key to all keys. It's more important to learn four moves and the twenty-four ways in which you can rearrange them."
- Ed Parker

"A Black Belt is a White Belt who never Quit!"
- Author unknown to me but on my studio wall for many years

"Float like a butterfly, sting like a bee."
- Muhammad Ali

"I done wrestled with an alligator, I done tussled with a whale; handcuffed lightning, thrown thunder in jail; only last week, I murdered a stone, hospitalized a brick; I'm so mean I make medicine sick."
- Muhammad Ali

"Just hit the Bastard!"
- Rick Hughes & Jim Mitchell (often to my over-analysis)

"One must get comfortable with being uncomfortable."
- Nelson Monteiro (Friend / Brazilian Jiu-Jitsu Instructor)

"How do you spell Lose? W-I-N, that's right, we don't even know how to spell it."
- Orned "Chicken" Gabriel (Friend / Fight Coach / Kenpo Master)

"Now remember, when things look bad and it looks like you're not gonna make it, then you gotta get mean. I mean plumb, mad-dog mean. Cause if you lose your head and you give up then you neither live or win. That's just the way it is."
- Outlaw Josey Wales (Clint Eastwood – Actor)

"It is the wood that should fear your hand, not the other way around."
- Pai Mei character (Kill Bill 2)

"Aim Small, Miss Small."
- The Patriot (Mel Gibson – Actor)

"I live, I love, I slay, and therefore I am content."
- Conan the Barbarian (2011)

"F.E.A.R. – False Evidence Appearing Real."
- Unknown

"Make him miss then make him pay."
- Every Boxing Coach

"Fast feet equal fast hands."
- Every Boxing Coach & Rey Leal (Friend / Kenpo & Tai Chi Master)

"Train Hard, Fight Easy."
- Vince Soberano (Friend / Professional Muay Thai Fighter / Coach)

"The difference between an amateur and a professional is that the amateur practices until they get it right and the professional practices until they can't get it wrong."
- Mike Benge (Friend / Musician)

"Old fighters never retire; they just take more time between rounds."
- David Arnold (One of my Black Belts)

Barry Barker Training & Teaching Quotes:
"It doesn't take a sledgehammer to kill a fly."

"Don't go Fast until you can go Slow."

"Mind - Body - Spirit: Movement precision comes from good instruction that gives an intellectual understanding to the Mind followed by correct physical repetition to train the Body that is then expressed in a way that flows passionately from the Spirit."

"When competing or performing don't get nervous, get anxious."

"One must learn the mechanics before being set free from them."

"Guts and conditioning enhance skill and knowledge."

"The synchronization of Basics for maximum results is the essence of a movements Timing."

"The shortest distance between two points is not necessarily a straight line, but the most direct path."

"Fighting is like Christmas, as it is better to give than to receive."

Analogies and Metaphors

ANALOGY - A figure of speech that relates the idea of one subject with that of another. Describing something new by attributing it to something more familiar does this. For example: relating an upward elbow strike to answering the telephone, an inward elbow to looking at a wrist watch, or a more complex analogy relating movement to a written language. These could also be thought of as a movement homograph.

METAPHOR – A figure of speech by which a term is transferred from one object to another by implied comparison. For example, they hit like a truck, move like the wind, or are as fast as lightening. These can relate to any subject and are used extensively by martial arts teachers. Here are a couple of my favorites followed by a list of martial art related books that I have enjoyed, and where no doubt more wisdom can be found.

Explosive Characteristic of Kenpo
Like dynamite, Kenpo technique explodes instantly, not gradually exploding. Like a light switch, Kenpo technique lights up instantly, not gradually.

Tomato in a Blender mentality
The relentless and continuous striking potential contained inside Kenpo technique, and the attitude associated with it, as per Kenpo Master Rick Hughes.

Striking Power
Hit like a truck. The bumper of the truck (the weapon: hand, foot, elbow, etc.) touches the target but the mass, weight, acceleration, inertia, momentum, and alignment of the trucks body is what causes the damage.

The Language of Motion
The original version of this is attributed to Ed Parker as a correlation between movement and the written English language. My concept and explanation are slightly different and includes the spoken language as a component. See the *Mind* for a full discussion but here is the basic idea.

Physical movement like language can be spoken by even the uneducated to an effective degree and written at from an elementary to a highly educated level. To become trained in a language it is best to learn the alphabet and then build a vocabulary with words from that language. As this vocabulary increases, one can understand the application of grammar and sentence structure.

This educated capability combined with physical principles help to attain mastery of that language. When put together with one's innate talents it can then flow effortlessly. A master can demonstrate this language prowess instantly and unrehearsed.

They can say a sentence, tell a short or long story, write a book, or more than one. This mastery can be expressed through written and verbal means and is without the capacity for ignorance. A master of language does not stutter or search for words as his oratory flows effortlessly while connecting one right word to the next.

Through this language study the master can attain a deep level of understanding and insight that the ignorant could never imagine or know without similar effort and talent.

My favorite Martial Art related books:
Infinite Insights into Kenpo Volumes 1-5 by Edmund Kealoa Parker
Encylocpedia of Kenpo by Edmund Kealoa Parker
Book of Five Rings by Myamoto Musashi
The Art of War by Sun Tzu
Karate-Do My Way of Life by Gichin Funakoshi
The Tao of Jeet Kun Do by Bruce Lee
Zen in the Martial Arts by Joe Hyams
The Chronicles of Tao by Deng Ming-Dao
Bubishi - The Classic Manual of Combat by Patrick McCarthy
The Art of Breathing by Nancy Zi
A Tooth from the Tigers Mouth by Tom Bisio
Bushido – The Soul of Japan by Inazo Nitobe, Sidekick Publications

EGO

The view we have of our self that is known as "ego" is a force within every person that can drive us to accomplish tasks, help form our worldview, determine how we interact and relate with other people and so much more. One of the significant efforts, benefits, and lessons offered through martial arts is in controlling this powerful and uniquely human motivational force.

It defines our confidence and affects much if not all our behavior, the good and the bad. There is no doubt a genetic component to a person's ego with upbringing and life's path contributing positively and negatively.

Everyone has their own story with many seeking "experts" to analyze their egos and give them advice, or drugs. My non-Freudian discussion presumes and accepts the egos role as a driving force in many of life's decisions, opinions, and the motivations that result in our accomplishments, failures, and peace of mind, or lack thereof.

It's an important martial arts topic with these my personal observations, opinions, and recommendations as I am not formally trained in a mental health discipline. However, as an observer and participant in the human condition while running a martial art school for many years I have gained insights on understanding and nurturing the human ego.

The ego, especially the male ego (the female ego is no doubt beyond a man's comprehension), is interesting to me as a teacher of fighting where confidence is of paramount importance. Male and Female egos cover the full spectrum from spectacular to dysfunctional, with a discussion of it able to leave one's own ego feeling vulnerable, or perhaps a little exposed.

A martial artist's goal (and a teacher's goal for students) should be in becoming a confident and skilled person with an indomitable spirit regulated by a humble ego. As a teacher (and parent) I have observed how the human ego benefits from martial arts training and how an insecure or undisciplined ego can be harmful to the person and society.

The ego it seems can be attached to good and not so good qualities in different people, or even in the same person at various times, with varying degrees of good and bad.

The good and not so good, or bad qualities, can seem to overlap when it comes to the human ego. Pride for example can be displayed as arrogance (bad) or after a productive accomplishment (good). Confidence can be displayed with cockiness (bad) or accomplished humility (good). This is the line the ego balances upon where pride without arrogance is encouraged and confidence without humility is intolerable.

Ego is closely related to self-esteem and a quality able to drive someone's spirit and passion towards accomplishing goals. This motivation can be felt as an introspective force fueled by personal motivation or a competitive energy directed towards our self or against a real or perceived adversary.

This motivation can have good or bad consequences. The bad is on display every day on the road where a driver's ego can cause choices to be made that they may regret later. An ego can feel challenged by another driver's positioning or speed causing competitive feelings towards them. This negative quality of our ego can result in fights if disrespect is intended or taken (road rage). They also can result in accidents and at the least is a cause of stress.

Performing or demonstrating in front of others and public speaking are other areas where otherwise sound people can become totally distracted or even dysfunctional as some will freeze up, walk / run away from such pressure. This fear is crippling for these people.

These insecurities in the ego come from a perception that other people are judging us, or that their motivation for observing and making decisions revolves around us and not them self. Whether true or not when/if we let others have this power over us then our egos are no longer under our control and we become susceptible to manipulation or are held back from progressing on our life's path.

This ego or internal force is at the core of what pushes us forward or holds us back. Our ego is more developed if and when we become mature and confident in our own skin. This then allows us to benefit from an occasion to perform, demonstrate, or speak in public, rather than run away from these personal growth opportunities.

This relates to martial arts because others can put themselves negatively in our path no matter how we try to avoid them. If this leads to a physical confrontation a determined self-centered ego is needed to achieve victory, but the ego should not be the reason for fighting.

Reasons for fighting can play out individually or on a global scale with a perceived wrong seen as "fighting words." Putting aside global terror, political aggression, and criminal assault the main reasons individuals get into street altercations are respect, pride, revenge, jealousy, intimidation, anger, and for some enjoyment, all based upon feeding the ego.

This is different than being in the military or working in law enforcement where, ego aside, a person's job leads them into an altercation.

Background is another variable that can lead a person from one culture, ethnicity, neighborhood or upbringing to react violently to something faster or slower than another person with a different background.

All these are variables a calm controlled ego can recognize and use to avoid or resolve a conflict before it escalates or decide to fight and be fully righteous in the effort, if that is the right choice.

Sport fighting motivation includes any or all the street fighting reasons but hopefully more often for the competition, or a way to test oneself, to grow as an athlete and person, and possibly for the camaraderie that can develop in these environments.

Sport is definitely a better outlet for someone's fighting energy than street. The drive to be a competitive sport fighter could also include recognition, awards, fame, and for some money, all are rewards for the ego but hopefully only short-term as the effort builds and develops character.

Sport fighting is a socially acceptable way to release the aggressive fighting spirit many people have that comes with the added, if initially unknown, benefit of gaining humility through the process (controlled ego). This is a tremendous way to build character while testing and developing a skill set, all of which helps develop the humble yet confident ego we seek through martial arts.

Whether for street or sport, a confident determined ego is needed in a fight whether motivated by good or bad, as finishing and winning depends on this determined confidence. Ego and confidence alone have won many fights as a weaker ego may give up or get "psyched out" thereby losing confidence and the will, i.e. spirit to fight. This can happen regardless of physical ability, talent, or skill as the mind leads the spirit, and the body follows.

An interesting ego phenomenon is someone's perception that talent alone is more important than skill and training. The reality of course is Mind-Body-Spirit are in everything from martial arts to cooking, dance, making music, playing any sport, or doing any job.

There are of course smart people without an education (Mind), physically gifted and talented athletes without training (Body), and souls full of enthusiasm, determination and drive without an outlet (Spirit). The athletes and performers that are smart, talented, and motivated become the best in a field, the all-stars among other relatively talented and skilled people.

Another type of ego that exists is one with real or imagined talent that thinks and sometimes talks about how great they are, often with little or no success to show for it. Their imagination rationalizes they have nothing to learn so they don't seek guidance and may even wonder why others don't acknowledge their greatness, as it's so obvious to them. This ego can be seen on reality talent shows where there always seems to be some untalented people who think they're great and are surprised, or even shocked, when others don't agree.

Leaving those people to bask in their own glory, Mind-Body-Spirit grows best when developed together. Technique, training, and insight are what coaches and teachers everywhere give to whoever wants or needs it. If someone shows up with talent and natural gifts that is a bonus.

When little Bruce Lee showed up in his first martial arts class I am sure his teacher was silently pleased, and when Michael Jordan walked onto a basketball court that coach probably thanked the heavens (although he was JV as a HS sophomore because he was too short at 5'11"). Both however, and all of us need development to reach our full potential.

Even as beginner's Bruce Lee and Michael Jordan were no doubt better than most of the less talented people, some of whom probably had more training, but this ratio has its limits. In the real-world talent alone is not enough, drive alone is not enough, technique alone is not enough. Together these are the makeup of people at the highest level in an activity, with the super talents just becoming the superstars.

The ego and martial arts has a unique interaction. Men for example often believe and fantasize how they can beat up most or all other men, sometimes regardless of any training or background in that area. It is a strange phenomenon that I also felt as a young man and have observed in others for many years while running a martial arts business.

This fantasy is normal but with maturity it becomes a non-thought as confidence contained within a humble ego is respectful to all while not underestimating anyone. The more mature thought process fights only if forced or sport fights against like-minded and similarly trained opponents.

A skilled martial artist should not feel a need to prove himself, especially against untrained citizens (even if sometimes deserving) in the same way an old west gunslinger should not have picked duels with farmers.

Young men have often come into my facility with confident (cocky) egos anxious to show the world what great fighters and tough guys they are. As a teacher of martial arts and a business owner it is right to be cordial and helpful in directing them to where they can prove and improve themselves.

My experience is through training, knowledge, and practice at a facility where humility and respect are demonstrated by the teachers and expected of the students this brashness transforms into a deep internal confidence.

This becomes a controlled ego with underlying confidence that builds into a powerful focused mind with real skill to back it up, if needed. Some of the best martial art practitioners start out with this raw trait and are often the breed of athlete many martial art teachers colloquially call the "tough guys" and I refer to as "terminators."

These are the physically gifted and durable athletes with strong, determined, and confident egos. This type of person often ends up in military special-forces or certain areas of law enforcement. Some become accomplished sport fighters or professional athletes, and who unfortunately could also become the hardened criminals.

Not everyone has the genetic makeup to physically perform at the level of these "tough guy" types but confidence and ego are not exclusive to these qualities. Traditional martial arts have evolved methods that help develop a stronger mind by building the spirit so even a physically weaker person can become unbeatable mentally. This can make them formidable physically regardless of genetics.

The reality is that martial arts teacher's want some of these tough guy terminator types as students as they are good for system notoriety and credibility. With that said it is not easy to tell by looking at someone what their mental makeup is or what training has or will do for them.

There are some very tough looking people with very weak spirits who may be masking that weakness with an outward tough guy demeanor. There are also some average looking and even gentle acting people who are very determined, strong-willed, deceptively athletic, and/or very skilled.

There is for sure a physical component to fighting but the strong focused and determined ego that won't quit will usually win over a strong body guided by a weak mind. The goal of a martial art teacher or program should then be the development of the entire person by helping build the mind, body, and spirit to attain this unbeatable yet humble ego.

Fight coaches do this all the time by giving fighters challenges while also trying to protect them from being overwhelmed or beaten down. The best sport fighting coaches "bring fighters along" with level appropriate challenges to help them grow *will* with *skill* as they discover how to utilize their talents.

Even among trained martial artists some can let their skill, physical talent, and the respect they get overwhelm their sense of self and ego. It seems easy to become full of our self with talent, training, recognition, and perhaps some fighting success. Trained martial artists can also run the full range from the truly humble to the "legends in their own mind."

Practitioners with this ego are usually treated with respect to their faces but perhaps talked about less favorably behind their backs. In martial arts many of these self-promote or allow themselves to be advanced in rank ahead of a timeframe found in any other field where degrees are earned through some standardized process.

This ego is also in the non-martial art world, so it is a personality type we must often tolerate. For the martial artist with this trait we may wish their teachers had put their public ego in check a little better, but nature takes care of this in its own time as life humbles everyone eventually.

A teacher is not fully responsible of course but does have an obligation to students and society to try and give everyone the tools to not only help optimize genetic talents but realize personal potential. Helping develop and direct a strong spirit and determined ego in a way that maintains focus and confidence but with humility does this.

A martial arts facility gets the full spectrum from the outwardly arrogant to the timid and afraid. Taught and developed properly the arrogant ego is put in check so to not be displayed negatively to the world, while the timid ego is nurtured and protected. They meet somewhere in the middle.

The arrogant ego gains humility through training where the timid ego gains confidence through attainable accomplishments, earned successes, and deserved compliments. Both egos then have productive confidence and a stronger balance in all aspects of their lives. This controlling the egos negative traits can help avoid physical altercation much of the time.

A humble and controlled ego may not be someone's initial goal, but it is a common result as we learn the limitations that go with our new skill and developed talents. A good teacher will usually have a bigger picture of a student then that student initially has for themselves and will teach with the end in mind, just like raising children.

With intention from good teachers this development of the entire person through martial arts can be life altering. Students tend to copy the attitudes of their mentors making it imperative for teachers to act as they want their students to act, the same as in parenting.

Teachers are not perfect people, so this responsibility can feel like pressure that can test a teacher's ego and confidence. Most students, like children, in time gain a more fuller appreciation for the well-intended, if imperfect people, who were their teachers, mentors, parents, but who always had their best interests at heart.

This mutual appreciation between student and teacher or child and parent is potentially one of the human egos greatest and most satisfying accomplishments. These are all compelling reasons for martial arts teachers and coaches to give more than just fighting skill, and a reason for much of the tradition in "traditional" martial arts.

Whatever the developmental source of this unique human quality, the fact is that we all have and need our egos. It gets us through life's trials and tests, and it can also make us feel like the center of the universe. This is where humility can put our ego in check by reminding us that we may be the center of <u>our</u> universe but not <u>the</u> universe. That is reserved for God.

Our overall goal should therefore be to have a strong, developed, and confident ego while not becoming intolerable to others. Humility demonstrated by skilled people is the trait most worth emulating. This control of ego leads to a calmness that allows us to think under pressure and react without visible emotion. This makes one much more formidable if need be.

The following Lao Tzu quote eloquently explains the benefit of the calm controlled ego that warriors of ancient times discovered and strived for in a time when most fights were to the death.

"He who excels in combat is one who does not let himself be roused." "That the warriors of old flocked to peaceful hermitages to foster their martial skills is no paradox; they came to learn how to apply the secret of emptiness, how to ensure that the enemy's sword, though aimed at flesh, encounters void, and how to destroy the foe by striking with dispassion. Hatred arouses wrath; wrath breed's excitement; excitement leads to carelessness which, to a warrior, brings death. A master swordsman can slay ten enemies simultaneously by virtue of such dispassion as he is able to judge to perfection how to dodge their thrusts. A swordsman or an archer's aim is surest when his mind, concentrated on the work in hand, is indifferent to failure or success."

We are all works in progress but so long as the goal is to be humble yet confident and determined then everything else will take care of itself.

My Favorite *Confidence* picture from a then 15-year olds
2011 Black Belt Thesis (Ryan Strommer)

MIND-BODY-SPIRIT CONNECTION

Connecting mental memory (Mind) with the physical structure (Body) and a willing effort (Spirit) happens over time with intention and is best done with guidance to help move us closer to a balanced and harmonious interaction with the universe. Wow, that was deep, but not that complicated and nothing martial arts training cannot help in developing.

Many people, especially those involved with athletics, have heard the concept of muscle memory where, hopefully, *correct* repetitive motion becomes more fluid with time. Most also understand mental memory as how our mind creates synapses to learn and remember things.

Once established, muscle memory is retained for life, so it never goes away and even improves with repetition. This muscle memory is still present in the body even if dormant for an extended period, or when the mind forgets after being away from an activity.

For example, once learned we can never forget how to ride a bike or swim. These are muscle memory examples where the balance and buoyancy once learned cannot be unlearned. The same is true in martial arts. The technique may not be as precise, and conditioning may not be what it was, but the body still remembers how to move. Catastrophic injury aside, the body cannot not know what it once knew.

This phenomenon is an intangible that expresses what the mind and body have melded together through the spirit. Eventually the eyes see, and the body reacts ahead of mental thought, i.e. *Spontaneous Stage of Learning*, although the mind still assesses, adjusts, and makes moral choices, i.e. *Extemporaneous Stage of Learning.* This is a result and one purpose of repetitive training.

The practice of doing the same movements over and over develops muscle memory to where they become reflexive and do not need conscious thought to be used. The body in this way becomes trained to naturally react in response to a stimulus. This correct repetition is the same in learning any physical skill from gymnastics to playing the piano.

Before this automated response can take place however mental memory needs to want to learn. The spirit is just the driving force that fuels the development of this reactive and reflexive muscle memory. This mental connection is a key component needed to understand and direct the body through correct repetition and eventually into muscle memory.

Since form does not come out of chaos without order it takes the mind to analyze, understand and direct our intention through proper technique, or the muscles would produce chaotic and nonsensical motion with no purpose. This presumes a student is getting knowledgeable instruction from a teacher who understands the skill being developed. This guidance eventually results in a reactive physical understanding.

An observable phenomenon for long time martial arts teachers is when students return after being away from training, yet their body knows moves their minds have long forgotten. Students who have not practiced for a time often have memory anxiety because they don't remember some movements and especially patterns that were learned previously.

The real phenomenon is that once in motion the revelation is that their body remembers what it had learned previously, which can be liberating and reassuring. That is of course until the mind starts analyzing and trying to remember then the body gets stuck again.

This Mind-Body-Spirit connection does not develop the same in all students. With children for example I recommend focusing on muscle memory first by helping them be in position for correct movement and alignment. I have felt like a puppeteer many times guiding children through movements but have found that to be the quickest way to develop good mechanics in them. This then becomes the muscle memory their minds will eventually connect with.

Since children generally do not have much existing muscle memory they are more pliable and easier to mold. However, with little existing muscle memory it can seem difficult to teach some children basic skills so helping them feel the alignment of movements while keeping intellectual descriptions simple works best, from my experience.

The way to get intention, enthusiasm, and martial spirit from children's movement is to tap into their imaginations by helping them fantasize about something exciting like being a ninja or tiger or some such thing. This with energy and a smile generates the energetic martial spirit sought.

Teens and especially adults have existing muscle memory from years of sports, other activities, or very little, so mental memory and intellectual analysis is engaged much earlier, the "whys" and "how's." This gets them on board with developing new muscle memory skills using their own minds to build upon, improve, and change existing bad movement habits.

The adage about "teaching an old dog new tricks" is true in many cases. A determined person overcomes these limitations to the best of their abilities and will show significant improvement relative to where they started. The key for them is "emptying their cup" to accept new movement methods.

Children can be nurtured and molded never knowing not being skilled or coordinated. Both eventually gain a more fuller understanding that makes martial arts about more than just exercise and fighting.

In both cases this can become the lifetime fascination with martial art technique and training that many of us have. This all starts with developing our self and possibly helping others to develop a Mind-Body-Spirit connection.

NUTRITION BASICS

This is a major subject as it affects our health and that affects everything we do. Without good health nothing else matters and life is less enjoyable. Our desire to train, learn, and become skilled at martial arts would become impossible without energy and health.

Even though we don't have full control over everything that can and will happen to us we should still be giving ourselves the best chance for optimal health. Accidents or illnesses can happen with much of our health determined by genetics, along with an ongoing and evolving constitution that is affected by our lifestyle, habits, biological age, etc.

We should be trying to avoid things that can deteriorate or poison our body. "All things in moderation" is good old-fashioned advice when it comes to having a long healthy life. Enjoy life and be happy but know, or at least recognize limitations by avoiding drugs, excessive alcohol, and not putting smoke into your lungs. Eliminate or minimally take in processed foods, sweets, sodas, etc., but anything can be bad if done to excess.

Traditional Chinese Medicine (TCM) has a wonderful and simple concept to explain the big picture of individual health called "Pre-Nata Qi" and "Post-Natal Qi." *Pre-Natal Qi* is what we are born with, our constitution, or the genetic makeup passed on to us by our biological parents. *Post-Natal Qi* is affected by what we or other people put into our bodies after we are born. This consists of the air we breathe, the liquids we drink, plus the foods and supplements we eat.

There is nothing we can do to control, determine, or affect the genetics we are born with, so managing our own health begins at Post-Natal Qi (future parents do affect the health of their unborn children however). When we are children our parents have the primary role in determining what we put into our bodies, then into adolescence we gain more control and then in adulthood we take over that primary role.

An important consideration is not only <u>what</u> we put into our body but also <u>how</u> our body receives, processes, and utilizes it. The air we breathe should be of good quality, but it also needs to be directed by good breathing technique (See *Breathing* in the *Mind*). The liquids, food and supplements we ingest should be nutritious, but our digestive system must absorb the nutrients for us to gain the benefit. (See *Digestive System* in the *Body*).

Understanding and helping our body have the capacity to fully absorb nutrients along with knowledge of how to correctly breathe in quality air is our lifetime responsibility and critical for us in managing our own health and maintaining a healthy Post-Natal Qi.

With good air, fuel, and building blocks absorbed into our body we have the energy, mental focus, physical strength, durability, recovery capability, and enthusiasm to thrive and develop throughout our lifetime in martial arts and other endeavors.

A lack of quality Liquids/Water and Solids/Food/Supplements will surely lead to poor health. Without quality liquids we can experience dryness or even dehydration symptoms ranging from minor to life threatening. Without healthy solids our body would not have the energy or building blocks needed for growth and repair.

Many sources of information exist surrounding this subject with many opinions and recommendations for anyone interested. The discussion here is an overview that covers the primary components and basic elements of nutrition, along with some essential information, and a few opinions.

Liquids

Water has a special unique quality in that it is "H2O" or 2-parts hydrogen and 1-part oxygen. This also means there is no "C" or carbon in water. Granted all water is not the same with variables such as distilled, deionized, spring, purified, etc. That aside, any other drink or solid has some Carbon ("C") elements meaning the stomach must digest it and other body systems must filter it. The cells can therefore absorb water without competing with other systems or functions.

In Western medicine and nutrition different thoughts exist on the recommended amounts of water needed daily based upon formulas using a person's body weight, or exerted energy, or the environment they are in, etc. In eastern medicine and nutrition, the amount of water needed daily is much simpler as it is determined by whether we feel thirsty. In either case the body will use the water it needs and get rid of the excess.

Water makes up about 60%-70% of our body as it flushes impurities from our systems, brings nutrients to our cells, and keeps our passageways to the outside moist. Without water we would begin to dry out and dehydrate, which would then lead to many more serious health issues.

When working out and training heavily however we need more than just water to maintain our energy level and keep our tissue nutrient rich. Water can be enhanced to keep us going, help us avoid injury and illness, make for faster recovery, contribute to repair of old damaged tissue, and build up new healthy ones. Even with all the various drink options available, water is still the base that all natural and man-made liquids, including sports drinks, are built upon.

During heavy sweating our body burns not only water but the "electrolytes" needed for physical and mental energy. If only water is used to replace that lost sweat our Central Nervous System (CNS) can be negatively affected causing water intoxication where water has replaced needed nutrients in our cells.

An electrolyte is an electrically conductive salt substance within our body that must be in proper balance for our physiology to function at its best. The electrolytes in the human body are sodium, potassium, calcium, magnesium, chloride, phosphate, bicarbonate, and sulfate, with sodium and potassium the electrolytes lost most during cardiovascular training.

—

Water is still the base element of all liquids we drink but electrolytes and other carbons can help us get the most out of our training. Carbon elements in our drinks can also include synthetic and natural sugars, vitamins, minerals, amino acids, etc. They can be customized configurations, or store bought pre-packaged drink mixes we blend together, or complete pre-mixed products that we purchase.

Solids

Proteins, Carbohydrates, and Fats are the commonly known food components that make up our body's nutritional needs and are covered here under "solids" but that can also be liquefied.

Healthy men and women are slightly different in their recommended percentages of these components, with women having more fat so needing a little more. A rough average is that Men need about 30% Proteins, 60% Carbohydrates, and 10% Fats; Women need about 30% Proteins, 55% Carbohydrates, and 15% Fats. These are only guidelines recommended by "experts" so they are open to debate.

In Western nutrition this energy in our body is measured in "calories" with food measured in "kilocalories" but generally just called "calories." A calorie is measured by how much energy is required to warm one gram of water by 1°C or 1.8°F.

A gram of protein and a gram of carbohydrates each contain 4 calories, but a gram of fat contains 9 calories. Knowing how many grams of protein, carbohydrates, and fats are in a food can help us calculate how many calories are in that food. This information can then be used for several reasons ranging from weight loss to weight gain, and even when trying to "make weight" in order to fight competitively.

It's estimated that an "average" adult needs about 2,000 calories each day for energy and for things to work properly. This presumes also burning about 2,000 calories per day. This estimate can vary greatly based upon someone's body dimensions, metabolism, and level of physical activity. People can become overweight when their calorie intake is greater than their calorie burn rate over time.

These calories are obtained from the foods we eat or from our body's reserves, which also come from the foods we eat. *Nutrition Facts* labels on packaged products show grams of proteins, carbohydrates, and fats, along with other basic information (see sample).

Proteins are essential to the growth and repair of muscle and other body tissues while also providing the enzymes that trigger chemical reactions in our body. Body proteins are either fibrous, forming the structure of our physical tissue, or globular, with many roles such as forming Enzymes and Amino Acids.

Enzymes are biological catalysts, or keys numbered in the thousands that can unlock complex compounds to create a chemical reaction. They are used to build things up and take things apart at a cellular level and are made from amino acids.

Digestive enzymes (probiotics) are very critical to the absorption of nutrients from food so many people take them as supplements, since enzymes cease to function after high temperature cooking.

Nutrition Facts

Serving Size 172 g

Amount Per Serving

Calories 200	Calories from Fat 8

	% Daily Value'
Total Fat 1g	1%
Saturated Fat 0g	1%
Trans Fat	
Cholesterol 0mg	0%
Sodium 7mg	0%
Total Carbohydrate 36g	12%
Dietary Fiber 11g	45%
Sugars 6g	
Protein 13g	

Vitamin A	1%	•	Vitamin C	1%
Calcium	4%	•	Iron	24%

*Percent Daily Values are based on a 2,000 calorie diet. Your daily values may be higher or lower depending on your calorie needs.

NutritionData.com

Amino Acids are left after proteins are digested so are organic compounds that also combine to form proteins. They are classified into two groups and, with some minor variables, are divided into 10 "Essential Amino Acids" and 10 "Non-Essential Amino Acids."

Essential Amino Acids cannot be made by the body and must be supplied through food. Sources include fish, meat, poultry, cottage cheese, peanuts, lentils, etc. Non-Essential Amino Acids are made from *Essential Amino Acids* in the body through normal protein breakdown.

10 "Essential Amino Acids" (with feature notes)
Aspargine (Not always Essential) – CNS, Immune & Healing
Histidine (Not always Essential) – (generates Histamine) Blood
Isoleucine – Muscles
Leucine – Blood, Muscles, and Hormones
Lysine – Helps the body absorb Calcium
Methionine – (generates Cysteine) Liver fat and collagen
Phenylalanine – (generates Tyrosine) Endorphins
Threonine – (generates Glycine & Serine) Tooth enamel and Collagen
Tryptophan – (generates Niacin & Seratonin) Nervous system
Valine – Muscles

10 "Non-Essential Amino Acids" (with feature notes)
Alanine – Glucose to energy
Arginine – (essential for children) Immune System & Muscles
Aspartate – CNS & Brain

Cysteine – (essential for children) Skin & hair
Glutamate – Brain
Glutamine – Brain
Glycine – (generates glutathione) Body protein
Proline – Collagen & Elastin
Serine – Blood sugar
Tyrosine – (essential for children) Thyroid

Carbohydrates are the main source of energy or fuel that our body's use. There are two types called "Simple" (simple sugars) and "Complex" (starches). The body breaks these down with enzymes to form glucose, a form of sugar carried in the blood to cells for use as energy.

After our body breaks down these carbohydrates into glucose any leftover glucose is stored as "glycogen" in our muscles and liver for later use. The body can only store so much glycogen so any extra is converted and stored as fat in the body.

This stored glycogen is the main source of fuel used by our muscles and enables us to do the aerobic and anaerobic activities we enjoy. Glycogen deficiency makes us feel tired and more prone to injury and illness.

Simple Carbohydrates, or sugars, are a necessary and fundamental fuel that our brain and body need to function, but since they are sweet and not bulky they not only taste great but are more easily eaten in greater volume than many complex carbohydrates, or starches. They are found in refined sugar products like cakes, some cereals, juices, soft drinks, jams, honey, etc. These simple sugar carbohydrates are also higher in fat.

Complex Carbohydrates, i.e. starches are bulkier and found in whole grains, vegetables, fruits, beans, potatoes, rice, bread, yogurt, etc. In addition, these starchy carbohydrates contain vitamins, minerals, proteins, and dietary fiber, while also being low in fat.

Fats and **Oils** are needed for maintaining healthy skin and hair while providing insulation for the body that helps us maintain normal body temperature and promote healthy cell function. Fats come in solids and oils with neither dissolving in water, meaning they can accumulate in the body if ingested to excess.

Fats and oils break down in the body to form glycerol and fatty acids, which are a valuable source of energy that is especially important in relation to the fat-soluble vitamins (A, D, E & K).

Fats are divided into "Saturated" (fats) and "Unsaturated" (oils). *Saturated* fats become solid at room temperature and come from animals. *Unsaturated* fats remain liquid at room temperature and come from non-animal sources. Saturated fats come from beef, bacon, cheese, butter, etc. Unsaturated fats from sunflower oil, olive oil, rice oil, nuts, fish, etc.

Trans Fats are another type of fat but are primarily man-made unsaturated fats used by the fast food and snack food industry, mostly because of the increased shelf life it gives their products. This manipulation of mother-nature is not surprisingly very bad for us, so these should be avoided when possible.

Triglycerides are a type of fat stored in the blood to be used later as a source of energy. Unused calories are converted into these triglycerides then stored in fat cells to be released as energy between meals. That is unless we consume more than we burn, in which case it can accumulate in our bloodstream becoming a health risk by clogging our arteries.

Cholesterol is a waxy cell building block produced by the Liver and Intestines that is also in our blood. Cholesterol is an essential element in our body but, like Triglycerides, if in too large a quantity can build up in our blood vessels and eventually cause life threatening health problems.

Dietary Fiber or roughage is another very important component in any healthy diet. It is the indigestible portion essential to having a healthy digestive system. This dietary fiber can be found in fruits, vegetables, nuts, seeds, wheat, whole grains, etc. Some dietary fibers also contain carbohydrates, but they primarily clean our digestive tract.

Many illnesses and conditions can evolve if our digestive system does not get rid of the old food products we ingest. This accumulation of old and undigested food grows in mass and ferments inside our stomach, small intestine, large intestine, and colon. This fermentation then generates heat that causes degeneration inside these tissue areas. This will eventually lead to major health problems. For these and other reasons having roughage or *Dietary Fiber* is a necessary part of any healthy diet.

Supplements
Supplements are the additional products taken or added to food or drinks to address a real or perceived shortage in the body. This is a general overview as many sources exist for those interested in learning more about this subject. Briefly covered here are "Vitamins," "Minerals," and "Enzymes" (Amino Acids was covered previously).

Vitamins play a vital role in the chemical processes of the body and must be obtained from what we eat and drink, or by taking supplements. They are divided into "Water Soluble" and "Fat-Soluble" types.

The water-soluble vitamins do not remain in our system so can be taken without problem as the body will use what it needs then dispose of the rest. The water-soluble vitamins consist of the 8 B's and Vitamin C.

Water-Soluble Vitamins (with feature notes)
- B1 Thiamine – energy metabolism, nerve function, muscle control
- B2 Riboflavin – use of fat, protein, and carbohydrates

- B3 Niacin – healthy skin and nervous system
- B5 Pantothenic Acid – helps cholesterol & reduces stress/anxiety
- B6 Pyridoxine – normal immune and nervous system function
- B7 Biotin – protein metabolism, glucose process, hair, skin, nails
- B9 Folic Acid – produces antibodies & helps maintain nerve tissue
- B12 Cobalamin – produces antibodies & nerve tissue maintenance
- C Ascorbic Acid – helps form collagen for tissue growth & repair

Fat-soluble vitamins can accumulate in the body so too much can lead to health problems. The fat-soluble vitamins are A, D, E and K.

Fat-Soluble Vitamins (with feature notes)
- Vitamin A – healthy mucous membranes & vital for good vision
- Vitamin D – from foods & the sun it helps the bones use calcium
- Vitamin E – antioxidant protects blood cell membranes & breaks fat
- Vitamin K – essential for blood clotting

Minerals are inorganic (not living) elements that make up about 4% of the human body and must be taken from outside sources. They are critical to normal body function and development as they provide structure, help maintain muscle contractibility, and regulate cell metabolism. The soil where plants containing minerals are grown is a factor in them being transmitted through food, making supplements useful for many people.

They are divided into "Major Minerals" (diet requires 100mg or more each day) and "Trace Minerals" (diet requires less than 100mg each day). These can be brought into our body through water, rooted plants, and animals. Listed are the 6 *Major Minerals* and 9 of the many *Trace Minerals* used and needed by the human body.

6 Major Minerals (with feature notes)
Calcium: Important for strong teeth and bones, and for muscle and nerve function. It is the major mineral constituent of bone. *Sources:* milk, yogurt, cheese, salmon, sardines, turnips, mustard greens, tofu, almonds, and broccoli.

Chloride: Regulates body fluid volume, concentration, and acid-base balance. Its balance is intertwined with sodium. *Sources:* see Sodium

Magnesium: Mainly inside muscles, soft tissues, and bone. It functions in many enzyme processes. *Sources:* nuts, legumes, whole grains, and green vegetables.

Phosphorus: Essential to bone formation and maintenance, energy metabolism, nerve function, and acid balance. *Sources:* meat, poultry, fish, eggs, dairy, and cereal products.

Potassium: Essential for nerve function, muscle contraction, and maintenance of normal blood pressure. *Sources:* fruits and vegetables.

Sodium: Regulates body fluid volume, concentration and acid-base. *Sources:* table salt (sodium chloride), foods processed with table salt, milk, milk products, eggs, and seafood.

9 of many Trace Minerals (with feature notes)

Chromium: Important in regulating blood glucose. *Sources:* brewer's yeast, whole grains, and meats

Copper: Important for nerve function, bone maintenance, growth, blood formation, and the utilization of glucose. *Sources:* organ meats, seafood, nuts, and seeds.

Fluoride: Important to dental and bone health. Greatly improves resistance to cavities. *Sources:* fluoridated water, foods cooked in or containing fluoridated water, fish with bones that can be eaten, and tea.

Iodine: Essential for production of thyroid hormones and is used inside the nose to kill infections. *Sources:* seafood, iodized salt, and foods containing iodized salt.

Iron: An essential constituent of blood and muscle and important for the transport of oxygen. *Sources:* liver, red meat, egg yolk, legumes, whole or enriched grains, and dark green vegetables.

Manganese: Important for growth, reproduction, bone formation, plus bone and carbohydrate metabolism. *Sources:* whole grains, fruits, vegetables, and tea.

Molybdenum: Involved in many enzyme processes, nerve function, and protein metabolism. *Sources:* milk, beans, breads, and cereals.

Selenium: Associated with antioxidant properties and fat metabolism. Caution: Taking excessive amounts of selenium may cause hair and nail loss. *Sources:* seafood and organ meats.

Zinc: Involved in wound healing, taste sensation, growth, sexual maturation, and part of many enzymes that regulate metabolism. *Sources:* meat, liver, eggs, and seafood (oysters).

Sulfur: Especially the organic sulfur compound MSM (methylsulfonylmethane) is an essential nutrient that helps slow aging and improves recovery of body tissue and fights inflammation. *Sources:* brussel sprouts, garlic, onions, kale, legumes, etc.

Other Trace Minerals include Cobalt, Boron, and Chromium.

Summary:

Everyone needs to stay hydrated with an individual's nutrition needs customized to that person and their goals. Body builders need different nutrition than distance runners for example. Building muscle mass requires more protein before and after working out where endurance athletes need more carbohydrates before and after.

Martial artists are a balanced combination of strength, flexibility, and endurance so, before and after training meals, should include a healthy balance of proteins and carbohydrates.

Nutrition is a vast and often controversial subject. Listen to coaches and those who seem knowledgeable but study the information and listen to your own body as individual needs vary, or can be completely and uniquely different, as are each of us.

Here's a simple baseline from which to build your unique nutrition needs.

Pre-Workout: The body needs carbohydrates to have energy, and protein to keep tissue strong and regenerating. These should be digested and out of the stomach at least 20-30 minutes by a workout start time, or as part of a liquid supplement.

During Workout: Stay hydrated. If sweating profusely, replacement fluids should have electrolytes.

Post-Workout: Lean fast-acting proteins help with quick recovery while ingesting a smaller percentage of carbohydrates than was needed pre-workout, and since less energy is needed after working out.

EXERCISE BASICS

This subject is under Spirit because knowing the what, how, and why of exercise can keep us motivated towards fitness, which keeps us showing up and participating. Knowledge in this area helps to avoid injury and the yearly gym phenomenon of people motivated to workout in January but who give up by March because they get bored and often frustrated from not knowing what to do.

Martial artists as athletes should never get bored because there is always something new to learn and improve upon, with fitness a key ingredient to continual development for athletes in any physical discipline.

The three main broad categories of exercise are *Endurance, Strength,* and *Flexibility*, which can be focused upon individually or in combination. "Common exercise wisdom" may change and fitness fads will come and go but all exercise falls under these main categories in some way.

A key factor when determining an exercise routine is our personal health matrix. This includes our constitution, body type, overall health, available time, talent, interest, and goals of training. Any discussion about exercise will have varied opinions and recommendations from all levels of experts and sources.

However, nobody knows us like we know ourselves so listen, ask questions, confirm through research, then add some common sense while considering your own personal health matrix. The only agreed upon constant with exercise is that we should not be injuring ourselves, and perhaps that we enjoy the process, or at least the result of the process.

Discomfort and even some misery are ok and perhaps even necessary to achieve any high-level of fitness, especially for competition. In any case, avoiding injury means the mind should stay focused, and there should be no internal organ pain, with no burning sensations or sharp pains inside the muscles, or at the attachments.

Pushing through a fresh or unprotected injury should be avoided, although in a competition environment this is often done or perhaps even expected. That's ok to a point so long as those injuries are well secured and protected and not made worse, then are immediately treated when the competition is completed.

Endurance, Strength, and *Flexibility* are covered separately here but have a huge overlap within and among them. In other words, muscular work raises the heart rate affecting endurance, and endurance work challenges muscle groups, with both engaging flexibility through various ranges of motion. The Warm-Up before and Cool-Down after is also important and briefly discussed.

Endurance refers to *Cardiovascular* (heart pumping and blood quality), *Respiratory* (air intake and expiration capability of the lungs), plus *Muscular* longevity (strength level over time) and recovery potential. Endurance exercises develop "aerobic" and/or "anaerobic" capacity.

Aerobic means "with oxygen" and refers to developing the lung capacity and arterial structures to freely move oxygenated blood so the body's cells can utilize it as this blood flows to challenged body parts.

Aerobic exercise strengthens the heart and lungs while burning fat. This is what a marathoner needs in order to run long distances.

Anaerobic means "without oxygen" and refers to how the body uses glycogen to fuel the muscles for speed, strength, and power. This is covered mostly in the section on strength, but this type of endurance is limited to the amount of glycogen stored in the body so athletes needing more of it will carb load to store more fuel before competing.

Anaerobic exercise builds lean muscle mass while burning calories in the body. This is what a sprinter needs for racing using short explosive bursts of energy. Lactic acid builds up quickly during this type of activity, so hydration is extra important to keep the muscles working effectively.

Most martial artists practice a combination marathon and sprint with aerobic and anaerobic activity in one. Tai Chi would be the aerobic extreme with the Sanchin Kata at the anaerobic extreme, but with most falling in between.

A martial artist training for a competition, a test, or a performance would want to increase both. This preparation builds to peak on "fight night" or whatever is being prepared for. This increased capacity for work is accomplished over time as we get "in shape," and then hopefully maintain it.

Methods for building endurance can range from jogging to sprinting, or interval training where jogging and sprinting are alternated. Other methods could include bike riding, swimming, hiking, and of course martial arts either in the air, on targets, or with a partner.

These get the heart beating faster, increase respiration, and challenge the body's structures. More oxygenated blood then moves into the cells of challenged tissue as the body builds into a more sustainable performance.

These efforts can be done to different degrees as we push our self or are pushed by a coach, trainer, instructor, or training partner through hard workouts. It is important in any case to start with good nutrition, stay hydrated, and don't allow your heart rate to get too high, so always listen to your body.

—

Strength here refers to muscular strength using Western terms to describe their function and development. This is anaerobic fitness, with the focus of this section on the methods to develop the muscular structure.

When applying force using the muscular system the reverse breathing technique is used (See *Breath* in the *Mind*). This creates the internal compression along with the organ system and core structural stability needed to develop explosive speed, strength, and power. Even though a muscle only contracts, there are two distinct types of muscle contractions.

A *concentric* muscle contraction is when a muscle shortens as it contracts, where an *eccentric* muscle contraction is when a muscle lengthens as it contracts. The shortening muscle is called the *agonist* with its paired lengthening opposing muscle called the *antagonist*.

A bicep curl with a weight for example is a concentric contraction (shortens) of the arms bicep muscle that occurs simultaneously with the eccentric contraction (lengthens) of the arms opposing tricep muscle.

This happens within the same muscle as well. A bench press is a concentric contraction (shortening) of the chest muscles (pecs) as the arms are straightened to push the weight away from the body but are an eccentric contraction (lengthening) of those same muscles as the arms are bent and the weight is lowered towards the chest.

In either case a muscle contraction is where the force generated by the muscle overcomes the resistance of a weight by pulling or pushing. A weight bearing motion does this along with an explosively accelerated movement that impacts a target then retracts, as done in martial arts.

Muscles work in pairs so not only does each muscle group need to be developed concentrically and eccentrically, the opposing muscle group must also be developed. An arms bicep curl (pulling concentric contraction followed by a pushing eccentric contraction) is balanced with a tricep extension (pushing concentric contraction followed by a pulling eccentric contraction).

The same is true with the lower body as the hip flexor contraction (pull) followed by a quad contraction (push) when doing a front kick would be balanced with a hamstring contraction (pull) and glute contraction (push) when doing a rear kick. Martial Art basics are very balanced in this way by design, with each also having reverse motions that become developed as part of the learning process.

Note: A common push/pull imbalance is forward or hunched shoulders. Chances are lots of weight has been pushed strengthening the chest muscles but not balanced with pulling exercises to develop the shoulders and upper back muscles. The result is short chest muscles pulling the skeletal structure forward stronger than the weaker back muscles can pull them back leaving unbalanced muscles, resulting in hunched shoulders.

Various methods and techniques are used to build balanced muscular strength. These all fall within the two categories of *Isotonic* and *Isometric* contractions.

Isotonic is where the tension remains unchanged as the muscles length changes by pushing or pulling against unchanging resistance through a range of motion (ROM). This is the common method done with weights, where it is usually done at a constant speed.

Elastic bands or weights (dumbbells) can be used to add resistance to the arms or legs as they move slowly through natural, useful, and sport specific ranges of motion. Whatever method is used form is important, so the correct muscle firing order can and should be felt. This increases muscle memory, extension, and strength through those motions without injury.

Isometric is a where muscle length remains the same against the tension. It's like holding a baby in your arms where the bicep muscle is concentrically contracted, but in place. The muscular force precisely matches the load and no movement results. This is what body builders do when they flex, and martial artists do when holding an opponent in place.

The three most popular methods practiced that build strength and challenge the muscles are *Dynamic Tension, Plyometrics,* and *Isokinetics.*

Dynamic Tension is the common name for a method to develop muscular strength that uses a blend of an isotonic and isometric contraction. Self-resistance is used by contracting muscles (Isometric), but while moving through a range of motion (Isotonic).

The name and technique are credited to the late Charles Atlas from the 1920's and is still a registered trademark of Charles Atlas Ltd. This method has however been used by martial artists since way before then to build muscle strength, flexibility, and endurance.

Engaging in Form/Kata practice and Horse Stance Basics are among the ways martial arts use to attain the benefits of *Dynamic Tension*. A well-known Form/Kata using this method is the "Sanchin Kata" from the Goju-Ryu System. Proponents assert this body hardening Form develops the muscular structure to where it becomes nearly impossible to injure.

Moving slowly with tension, whether doing the Sanchin Kata, or any other refined martial art movement, has the added benefit of developing muscular endurance through useful ranges of motion. Awareness of precise musculoskeletal mechanical alignment while applying correctly felt technique builds into refined and precise muscle memory.

Plyometric exercises challenge the stretch reflex of a muscle or group of muscles and could easily be listed under *Endurance* training. It involves a muscular explosion where rapid alternation of lengthening (eccentric contraction) and shortening (concentric contraction) of muscle fibers against resistance is used. Resistance can be natural body weight or enhanced with a weighted object.

Examples of *Plyometric* exercises would be jumping up onto a box where the legs push then rapidly pull; or pushups where the hands are clapped before they get back to the floor. Adding weight enhances these exercises such as jumping up on the box holding a medicine ball, or doing those pushups wearing a weighted vest, etc.

Plyometrics are used to develop speed with explosive power by compressing the force of a muscular contraction into as short a period as possible. This dynamic power is exactly what martial artists and especially strikers need and should strive to develop.

This more holistic muscle development approach uses multiple muscle groups simultaneously where traditional weightlifting focuses on building individually defined muscles and muscle groups.

Plyometric exercise does however put the greatest amount of stress on the joints and tendons, so it must be done correctly and not overdone. It may also not be suited to older athletes, or someone with an unstable joint, or an unhealed injury.

Isokinetic training is when constant torque or tension is applied in both directions as muscles shorten (concentric) or lengthen (eccentric) with either weight or a resistance force applied through a range of motion. This would be as opposed to working a muscle group in one direction then relaxing it in the opposite direction.

This is often done with equipment where steady pressure can be applied against the muscles through the pushing and pulling directions. Shadowboxing with dumbbells is an example where both the extension and contraction sides of the muscles are used. Standup grappling and clinch work with a partner or opponent also has elements of this.

Flexibility refers to the elasticity of the body's tissue that allows the muscles and joints to move through more extended ranges of motion. This is determined by the length and pliability of the muscles, tendons, and ligaments. It is improved upon using *Active / Dynamic / Movement Stretching* and/or *Static / Passive / In-Place Stretching*.

In both cases use the relaxed breathing technique (See *Breath* in the *Mind*) so the mind is calm, and the muscle fibers can relax and stretch.

—

Note: After an injury overstretched or torn muscle fibers begin to heal by laying down fibroblasts (new tissue) in random patterns that replace and repair what was "use specific tissue," but is now damaged.

To clarify, before the injury that tissue was organized in a direction designed for its specific use, but the new repairing tissue is laid down randomly and in different directions. This is referred to as "scar tissue" that needs to be broken down to eliminate the non-useful tissue leaving the directional muscle fibers as before the injury. Stretching, along with massage, is one of the methods that contribute to this healing and recovery process.

Active / Dynamic / Movement Stretching is when the musculoskeletal structure is moved through a natural range of motion. Arm circles, leg swings, opening and closing the arms in front of the chest (chain breakers), as commonly done at the beginning of a workout are common examples. These get the major muscle groups and attachments primed for an activity.

The flow of this loosening process can be totally random or organized. It could start at the head/neck/shoulders working down, or from the toes/feet/ankles working up or start in the middle at the hips/waist/back and move out. The goal is to loosen up the moving parts of the body.

Static / Passive / In-Place Stretching is maintained or held stretching, usually with natural body weight at the point of the stretch. Holding the feet apart as far as possible with the legs straight for example is a static stretch commonly called the "Chinese splits." The weight of the body pushes down causing the legs to be pushed (stretched) apart, which challenges the normal directional function to help increase muscle and attachment length, and therefore range of motion.

This can become more *active* by adding isometric tension to engage the stretched muscles in short bursts (10 seconds or less) to help develop more strength through those stretched muscles. Against a wall, a partner can help by pushing each limb up beyond where we could do it ourselves.

This static stretching is often done at the end of a workout to elongate muscles that have been shortened from vigorous exercise and weight training. Yoga enthusiasts, dancers, gymnasts, and some martial art styles do this to a sophisticated level.

Warm-Up and Cool-Down are important components to any fitness training. The body should go through at least a basic *warm-up* before moving to more intense exercise, and some time should be taken to *cool-down* when finished. Here are the basics of this vital component of fitness that is too often limited by impatience, time, or both, but still very important and should be included when possible.

Warm-Up is how a workout should start. Most martial art workouts start with some light whole-body movement. Bouncing and shaking out the joints, maybe jumping rope, jumping jacks, or a light jog to get the blood moving through the body in preparation for other warm-ups and more vigorous movement.

The "body slap" is a martial art warm-up where different areas of the body are slapped to prepare it for harder work and especially contact training. This stimulates the Qi, with the intensity of these self-slaps depending on the person and the area being stimulated. This would also include rubbing the skin with the palms to warm and invigorate an area.

Once the heart rate is elevated then moving the joints through major ranges of motion using *active stretching* can be done in any order, but all the joints should be moved. This would include moving the head, neck, shoulders, arms, elbows, wrists, fingers, waist, hips, low back (all directions), knees, ankles, feet, and toes. Some *static stretching* can also be added as needed for high use areas.

Large muscle groups should also be primed with natural body-weight strength exercises such as push-ups, sit-ups, and squats. Together these get the body ready for harder work.

Cool-Down is how a workout should end. This is the time at the end of a workout where we can help our body absorb the benefits we seek. It usually involves soft easy movements followed by light or perhaps more serious static stretching to elongate challenged muscles.

This is done while catching our breath, re-hydrating, perhaps adding some nutrition, and even spending some time socializing with colleagues.

Unfortunately, this cool-down is often skipped or eliminated due to available time at the end of a workout, but it is highly recommended that time be allocated for this component of fitness and health.

FOR PROFESSIONAL MARTIAL ARTISTS
Chapter V

This chapter addresses areas that the professional or lifetime martial artist may want to know and have a grasp of to a higher level than most. Like the previous chapter these subjects affect the enthusiasm or spirit at a martial arts facility. The areas discussed here are *Martial Arts First Aid, How to Teach Martial Arts,* and *The Business of Martial Arts.*

For the professional martial artist, the subject of First Aid is especially important for training safely and for knowing how to manage acute and chronic injuries. Students and training partners who are unable to train due to injury don't show up, slowing or stopping their progress, and those they work with, plus nobody likes being injured, and it's bad for business.

In the spirit (pun intended) of having that knowledge, effective treatment strategies for the most common martial art injuries are covered. Most are treatable without going to a doctor, which all the martial artists I have ever known, including myself, avoid if possible. Basic and some advanced information are given from both Western and Eastern medical model perspectives.

Of course, getting professional treatment is always recommended, especially for any injury resulting in loss of consciousness, loss of nerve function, or major loss of blood, bodily function, or mechanical ability. Injury treatments covered here however can provide insight and guidance.

How to Teach Martial Arts is covered because the longer you do martial arts the more likely you will be asked to teach others. Many discover they have some aptitude at this and want opportunities to teach, but the reality is that skill is relative, so anyone could be asked to teach. This section is also for those who just want to be better at teaching martial arts.

I do recommend teaching and require it around Brown Belt level for my students. The greatest gains in personal knowledge come through teaching others, with the bonus benefit of passing martial arts forward. The old saying "if you give it you keep it; if you keep it you lose it" is very much true.

The Business of Martial Arts is covered in a general way here but can give anyone considering martial arts as a profession, or someone already doing this, insight and the basics for running a successful martial arts business.

Tangible nuts and bolts are covered with some philosophical intangibles that are even more critical to staying in business for a long time and enjoying it. For those that this applies I wish you the best of luck as being a professional martial arts teacher can change lives for the better.

MARTIAL ARTS FIRST AID

This very broad subject is written here with the layperson in mind. My effort is geared towards common types of injuries that I have observed (and experienced) in martial arts, along with some treatment methods.

This is by no means a comprehensive work on first aid and healing but presented here is a lot of useful information from the Modern Western Medicine (MWM) and Traditional Chinese Medicine (TCM) perspectives.

I would be remiss if I did not recommend professional medical attention for the injuries discussed so consider it my recommendation to always seek professional medical attention, especially for serious injuries or worsening conditions. My experience is that martial artists generally avoid doctors and get professional help only if physically taken to the hospital, so this chapter can help.

Common Injuries covered are *Overuse, Bruises & Contusions, Sprains & Strains, Cuts & Abrasions, Concussions, Dehydration, Heat Exhaustion* and *Heat Stroke*.

External Treatment Methods covered are *Oils/Liniments/Creams, Ice, Heat,* and *Braces/Supports/Tape*. Internal Treatment Methods covered are *Chinese Herbs, NSAID's,* and *Homeopathic Remedies. Recovery Therapy* is also discussed.

Remember that injuries can be *acute* or *chronic. Acute* injuries are those that just happened and *Chronic* injuries ongoing, i.e. nagging injury. This often determines the type of treatment with the acute injury where expert advice and treatment is especially helpful and could even be critical.

COMMON INJURIES

Each of these will have a *Definition* that describes the condition, then common *Symptoms* followed by a basic *Treatment* strategy and any *Notes*. This information is not intended to replace professional medical advice but to give insight as to when and how to treat things on your own, and when to seek expert medical attention.

OVERUSE

Definition: This common injury happens mostly at joints and tendon attachments but can be deeper inside a joint capsule, or in a muscle structure. See "Sprains & Strains" for each joint. It occurs by doing the same repetitive motion(s) over and over to an extreme degree and/or incorrectly.

Repetitive and continual use of joints, attachments, and muscles can lead to irritation and eventually more permanent tissue damage. This irritation of the bodies moving parts results in limited movement or pain with movement and can affect any area where repeated movement occurs. Athletes often experience it in the shoulders, elbows, wrists, hips, knees, ankles, and sometimes the neck and back.

Symptoms: Pain, swelling, discomfort, limited strength and range of motion (ROM)

Treatment: The best treatment for overuse is rest. Wearing supports and braces to protect an injured area is useful if movement must continue. Therapeutic methods vary but generally try to limit initial swelling then bring new healing energy to the area. Rest is the key followed by slow rehabilitation, with Acupuncture very powerful in speeding up healing. Incorrect movement must also be corrected to help avoid further injury.

Note: There is no such thing as "tendonitis" since there are no inflammatory cells in tendon tissue, as they are made up of collagen and water. Body tissue is constantly degenerating and regenerating so an overuse injury is when degeneration is occurring faster than regeneration and called "tendonosis" or more severely "tendonopathy." This means the MWM treatment of injecting cortisone and using NSAID's does not help a tendon injury and may even cause more harm.

BRUISES & CONTUSIONS
Definition: A *bruise* refers to tissue damage under the skin where blood has leaked out of the blood vessels and become trapped between skin layers. This bleeding into the interstitial spaces of tissue is seen as a dark colored mark on the skins surface and may also be felt on the inside.

A *contusion* is a more serious bruise that is deeper inside the body at the level of the bone, tendons, and ligaments, or possibly even to an internal organ, although not as extreme as a break, tear, or rupture.

These are caused by heavy trauma to any part of our body from an opponent's body part, an external weapon, the ground, other hard environmental surfaces, or by over twisting. This is a good reason for wearing protective equipment where and when possible. Skin level bruises and deeper contusions can be seen and felt almost anywhere on the body. Martial artists commonly experience them in the following areas:

Forearm and Shins: These areas are often used to absorb impact, or they just bang against someone else's complimentary part (arm-on-arm or shin-to-shin). With the bones so prominent under the skin there is no padding for impact absorption making for an almost instant bone bruise.

Upper Arms and Thighs: The upper arms and thighs often must take hard kicks, or impact against a hard-unforgiving surface. This can result in a muscle and/or bone bruise.

Ribs and Intercostal Spaces: The ribs can be damaged from the trauma of being kicked, punched, crushed, or caused to twist. It is a vulnerable area that is very susceptible to injury in fighting sports and takes a while to heal. It's hard to protect and is an injury often felt with every breath for some time.

<u>Hip</u>: This joint and surrounding musculature are vulnerable to striking attacks or by impact with the ground. With its closeness to the core of our movement this type of injury can seem and be very debilitating.

Symptoms: Discoloration is, by definition, bruising but sometimes bruises cannot be seen. They may occur deeper inside the body and can extend beyond what is visible as they taper off under the skin.

Tenderness is another symptom of bruising, especially with deeper damage to muscles, bones, ligaments, or tendons. These are often felt but not seen, as with many contusions.

Treatment: Depending on the area Dit Da Jow (see *Treatment Methods*) and other blood moving liniments can be used. The healing strategy is to move the blood to bring healthy new cells to the area while aiding in removing old dead cells.

Light stretching of a bruised muscle or attachment could be done but only if the sensation felt is the "hurts so good" or achy type. There should never be sharp pain or burning when stretching a damaged area. Sport creams can be used to make the surface feel better and possibly help with healing by moving the Qi.

SPRAINS & STRAINS
Definition: When tissue is challenged beyond its normal range of motion to where damage occurs, yet everything is still connected. This can happen within a muscle where they connect to a bone at tendons across a joint, at ligaments where bones connect to each other, or within a joint capsule.

This is not a tear or rupture as those would require medical attention and probably surgery to repair, but this can occur from external trauma, hyperextension, twisting, or from overuse, and are inevitable in the life of a martial artist. Most relatively minor versions of this can be self-treated.

Muscles, tendons, and ligaments can contain thousands of individual fibers. Muscles are fired by Motor Units and attached by tendons that contain a Golgi Tendon Organ which protects the attached muscle from tearing. Tendons and ligaments are avascular (without blood) so are slow to heal taking 6-8 weeks, presuming no re-injury along the way.

However, if only a small percentage of these fibers become traumatized, overstretched, or possibly even torn, the surrounding undamaged fibers will still allow the muscle, tendon, and/or ligament to have some function.

This allows for semi-normal function, even though weakness, discomfort, and pain are felt at certain angles of use, or ranges of motion. Medical advice would be useful to determine the extent of injury but unless it requires surgery MWM is very limited. TCM has other techniques to speed up healing, some of which we can do on our self, once shown.

The following joints can be hyper-extended by traumatic impact or pressure. If an audible pop occurs as a joint is hit, pressed, or twisted this is a sign that the capsule has been damaged. Hyperextension can also be self-induced by over punching or kicking to where an elbow or knee joint extends past muscular control, potentially damaging the structure.

<u>Wrists</u>: This is the connection where the hand, wrist, and forearm work together allowing the hand to move into extension, flexion, radial flexion, ulnar flexion, external rotation, and internal rotation. This flexibility of hand movement also makes it a weak junction that is easily injured.

<u>Elbows</u>: This hinge joint can be hyper-extended (over straightened) or twisted through our own acceleration or someone else's leverage. The forearm muscles at the elbow attachments can be damaged or overused with pain felt at the inside elbow joint known as "Golfers Elbow" (medial epicondylitis) and on the outside known as "Tennis Elbow" (lateral epicondylitis). The joint capsule surrounding the joint can also be damaged along with the tricep attachment at the back of the arm.

<u>Shoulders</u>: This ball and socket joint allows for full rotation of the arm and hand making overuse injuries common. The wrist at the end of this lever arm can be moved, with a bent elbow, over (American lock) or under (Kimura lock) the shoulder line, putting severe stress on that joint.

Note: The Rotator Cuff is a group of tendons and 4 different muscles that allow for arm movement at the shoulder joint. The Supraspinatus is at the top of the shoulder with the Infraspinatus, Teres Minor and Subscapularis underneath.

<u>Low Back</u>: This Lumbosacral area of the back is a critical link in any effort involving lifting and explosive whole-body movement. Pain occurs from accidental injury or strain from overuse, and often from poor ergonomics. This occurs more as people get older, especially men over the age of 40, often doing something minor like tying their shoes or picking up something light. It can re-occur throughout life where simple movements cause a "pinched nerve" resulting in inconvenient, if not debilitating, back pain.

Poor ergonomics, posture, and body awareness while moving, often too fast, can be the cause of this as a repetitive injury. Bending at the waist disengages the legs, then rotating the upper body causes this injury. The mechanism is the spinal vertebrae's facet joints are negatively affected by this series of motions and can pinch a nearby nerve. To avoid this, always keep shoulders and hips aligned with each other when moving.

Another major cause is lifting heavy objects using the back instead of the legs. Remember, if your legs can't lift it, your back definitely can't! Back supports should be worn when doing heavy labor, especially over extended periods of time, and are also used to provide support after an injury.

<u>Knees</u>: The four main knee injuries are Patellar Tendon strain (Patellar Tendonosis); ACL (Anterior Cruciate Ligament) strain or tear; MCL (Medial Collateral Ligament) strain or tear, and a Medial Meniscus tear.

The *Patellar Tendon* is located just below the kneecap at the top front of the shinbone where it connects the shinbone over the knee to the quad muscles. Patellar Tendonosis or "runner's knee" is very common and in growing active children is called "Osgood-Schlatter Disease." Note: There is no such thing as "Patellar Tendonitis." See Overuse note.

The *Anterior Cruciate Ligament (ACL)* is one of two ligaments that cross at the back of the knee connecting the thighbone (femur) to the larger shinbone (tibia) to help stabilize the knee. An ACL tear is caused by hyperextension and/or twisting this tissue.

The *Medial Collateral Ligament (MCL)* is the inside ligament that holds the femur and tibia together. Forceful pressure at the outside of the knee can cause it to buckle inward causing this ligament to strain or tear and is a common football injury. Sudden inward movement without external force can also cause this damage.

The *Medial Meniscus* is located at the lower inside point at the front of the knee, beneath the small indention. It is damaged by landing forcefully, which compresses the meniscus padding between the bones, then rotating inward, causing the two bones to pinch this pad causing a tear.

Note: Athletic activity that requires unpredictable movement and acceleration is hardest on the knees. Often surgery is the best choice for those still wanting to compete and train hard. It is best to seek expert medical advice under these circumstances.

<u>Ankles</u>: Damage to the ankle can involve the joint line (like with the wrist), ligaments at the outside of the foot (rolled ankle), ligaments that connect the two lower leg bones (high ankle sprain), or the Achilles tendon at the back of the foot.

In conclusion these and other areas including upper or lower arms, the small bones and muscles of the hands and feet, and especially the neck can become injured. This can happen to all active people who do repetitive motions, and especially "weekend warriors" who participate without any or much preparation. When in doubt seek expert medical advice.

People experience twisted and rolled joints, but martial artists have the additional factor that an opponent could grab and intentionally bend or twist those joints to cause that trauma. All these are good reasons for body awareness, correct form, tapping out early in training, and practicing with controlled partners.

It's also important to warm up, stretch, and become familiar with our own ranges of motion. Kicking too high or hard for example without preparatory steps can result in damage like a hamstring, hip flexor, or groin strain.

Symptoms: Pain, tenderness, swelling, heat

Treatment: Rest is best! Control the initial traumatic inflammation but remember some inflammation is good as this is the body's natural healing and repair mechanism. As with *Bruises & Contusions* applying liniments like Dit Da Jow, sports creams, castor oil, or medicinal oil can help ease pain and speed up healing. Light movement stretching is also therapeutic, if with no sharp pain, although some achiness helps the tissue move towards healing.

CUTS & ABRASIONS
Definition: When a body-covering surface like skin is compromised or damaged in a way that exposes the internal body to the external environment. This involves cuts that open in a straight or curved line, puncture holes, or an abrasion where a larger skin surface is removed.

These become more serious if an infection develops. This then leads to other problems for the martial artist, their training partners, and the facility where they train. Staph infections, ringworm, and other dangers await practitioners and environments that are not clean.

These can affect any area of the skin and are often caused by training partners with unclipped finger and toenails, or from scraping the skin surface (often elbows and knees) along a floor surface (mats, carpet, etc).

Symptoms: If contained to just the skin then some pain, discomfort, and perhaps bleeding depending on depth, length, and width of the damage.

Treatment: Not exposing an open wound to the environment or other people is critically important to everyone's health. Clean and disinfect, apply some type of anti-biotic ointment, seal and cover with appropriate bandage or wrap. If bleeding cannot be stopped or the area won't stay closed (near a bone for example) professional medical attention is needed.

CONCUSSIONS
Definition: Any head trauma that results in unconsciousness, disrupted mental focus or brain function problems, as opposed to panic, fear, etc. This is bruising to the brain from impact against the skull bones and is something that happens often in contact sports like football and sometimes martial arts, especially full-contact sport martial arts, where the intention is to damage the opponent to win.

Note: Most sport fight athletes would not want to permanently hurt or cause the death of a sport opponent, but it can and has happened.

Symptoms: Unconsciousness, dizziness, nausea, headache, slurred speech, unfocused eyes, lack of concentration, balance problems, sensitivity to light, tired with no energy.

Treatment: Anyone who is knocked unconscious or made dizzy due to a head trauma or whose head hits the ground hard should get an examination and opinion from a qualified medical expert. They should then be monitored to assure more serious symptoms do not develop. Further concussion incidents <u>must</u> be avoided until the brain bruising has completely healed, at least 1 week and perhaps longer.

DEHYDRATION
Definition: A lack of fluid in the body, usually accompanied with excessive sweating. This often occurs in the heat while doing extreme exercise without enough rest or liquid nutrients containing electrolytes to keep the body systems functioning properly. This is fluid deficiency allowing the body to run hot, or a lactic acid buildup, or low potassium levels in the muscles.

Symptoms: Muscle cramps are the main initial symptom of dehydration. This is when muscles tighten up uncontrollably in a dramatic and drastic way. This can occur in any muscle, with calf cramping common since they are often being used extensively in these situations.

Note: Mental focus and low energy symptoms from dehydration are much more serious as they show a worsening condition that is moving from simple dehydration towards *Heat Exhaustion*, or even *Heat Stroke*.

Treatment: Stretch cramping muscle(s) to treat this symptom. Dehydration is a relatively minor condition but should be recognized and treated immediately by replenishing the fluids and resting in a cool place. The observation and treatment of *Dehydration* is critical to avoiding it becoming a much more serious condition.

HEAT EXHAUSTION
Definition: This more serious condition can stem from *Dehydration* if fluids are not replenished soon while cooling down and resting. The two main types of *Heat Exhaustion* are excessive thirst with headache and/or nausea with muscle cramps. Excessive thirst with headache indicates fluid depletion whereas nausea with muscle cramps are salt (electrolyte) depletion symptoms.

Symptoms: Confusion, dark urine, dizziness, fainting, fatigue, headache, muscle cramps, nausea, pale skin, profuse sweating, rapid heartbeat

Treatment: Get out of the heat!!! Rest, rehydrate, and cool down. Seek medical attention if not improving or if symptoms become worse.

HEAT STROKE

Definition: This extremely dangerous condition is more serious than *Heat Exhaustion* and can result in extreme health problems or even death. It can occur indoors but commonly happens in the heat of the sun. It results from over-training in the heat without enough rest, shade, and hydration. The body and mind begin to struggle keeping up with the demands being put upon it before eventually shutting down.

Symptoms: Throbbing headache, dizziness and light-headedness, lack of sweat, red hot dry skin, muscle weakness or cramps, nausea and vomiting, rapid heartbeat, rapid shallow breathing, disorientation, confusion, staggering, seizures, unconsciousness.

Treatment: Call 911 or take directly to a hospital emergency room. Give *Heat Exhaustion* treatment until professional medical help can take over.

TREATMENT METHODS

These are methods and strategies to treat common injuries that martial artists and all athletes can experience. They are divided into *External Treatment Methods* on the skin surface, *Internal Treatment Methods* taken orally, and *Recovery Therapy*.

External Treatment Methods include *Liniments & Creams, Ice, Heat,* and *Braces-Supports-Tape.* Internal Treatment Methods include *Chinese Herbal Medicine, NSAID's,* and *Homeopathic Remedies.* Recovery Therapy *covers Massage, Strength Building,* and *Stretching.*

This information is not intended to replace expert MWM or TCM advice and treatment, but it can provide insight into the major concepts for managing and healing non-emergency type injuries with basic self-treatment information. Use these methods at your own risk.

EXTERNAL TREATMENT METHODS
OILS - LINIMENTS - CREAMS
These are used for different types of injuries that are treated by applying an herbal solution or topical cream onto a damaged area. Most are used over a closed wound, but a few can treat open wounds externally, with some also internally.

These pre-made solutions can be purchased at drug or herb stores, or online. They are applied directly to the skin manually, or as a therapeutic wrap. They are mostly oil based, alcohol based, or manufactured creams. Each item listed has a *Description* with its *Function* followed by its *Purpose*, then any special *Notes* or *Precautions.*

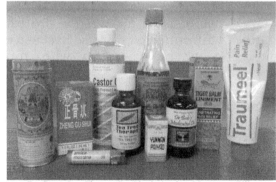

Po Sum On, Zheng Gu Shui, Arnica Montana Pills, Castor Oil, Tea Tree Oil, Dit Da Jow, Yunnan Pai Yao, Dr Bob's Medicinal Oil, Tiger Balm, Arnica Cream

Covered are Castor Oil, Dit Da Jow, Zheng Gui Tui Na, Zheng Gu Shui, Po Sum On, Thai Oil, San Huang San, Yunnan Pai Yao, Dr. Bob's Medicinal Oil, and Western Body-Ache Creams, including Tiger Balm.

CASTOR OIL

Castor oil has been used therapeutically internally and externally for hundreds of years. It's a vegetable oil obtained by pressing the seeds of the castor oil plant and is indigenous to the southeastern Mediterranean Basin, Eastern Africa, and India. When applied topically it has many beneficial effects for a wide range of conditions.

Castor oil consists of about 90% Ricinoleic Acid, an unsaturated omega-9 fatty acid. Such a high concentration of this substance is thought to be responsible for castor oils healing abilities. In real terms the bones, ligaments, tendons, and muscles like being soaked in Castor Oil, responding by feeling better and healing more quickly.

Function: It cools internal heat in the tissue and its moist properties lubricate and soften tissue, especially hardened scar tissue near joints.

Purpose: Speeds repair and recovery of musculoskeletal ailments or injury. TCM practitioners also use it as a pack on the Liver to calm the nerves and relax the spirit. Do your own research to know the many healing qualities attributed to Castor Oil.

Application (Castor Oil Wrap): This method applies Castor Oil to the skin easily in a way that allows for tissue absorption while not being too messy. Make the wrap using the ingredients below then apply to the affected area for 15-45 minutes (depending on skin sensitivity).

Needed: Plastic (saran) wrap; 4" gauze square; castor oil; hand towel; heating pad

Directions:
- ✓ Cut plastic wrap to fit around the size of area to be treated
- ✓ Open, refold or cut gauze to fit within the plastic wraps borders
- ✓ Pour castor oil onto the gauze (too much can get messy)
- ✓ Place plastic wrap, gauze, and oil onto affected area (oil towards skin)
- ✓ Place towel over the plastic wrap
- ✓ Place (warm) heating pad over towel (wrap with an Ace bandage)

Leave 15-45 minutes – check skin occasionally for sensitivity. If painful then remove immediately. When finished remove gauze by wrapping it inside plastic wrap and throw away. Wipe off skin with towel or another dry cloth. *This should feel good.*

Precautions: People with sensitive skin or certain body areas can become irritated so use for less time and perhaps with less heat. <u>Do not</u> use heat in this way if the area is already hot, swollen, or inflamed.

DIT DA JOW

Dit Da Jow is an alcohol-based bruise liniment commonly available at Asian markets and Chinese Herb stores. It's an external liniment designed to treat trauma injuries and bruises. The Asian martial arts community has used this classic formula, commonly known as "Hit Medicine," for centuries. It contains Qi and blood moving herbs that speed up the healing process and improve tissue integrity while relieving swelling and pain

This blood moving quality also makes it widely used to strengthen the tissue of the hands, feet, shins, etc. Practitioners who break boards or bricks especially will commonly use Dit Da Jow to prepare their bodies for this impact. Many martial artists apply this liniment to their shins, feet, forearms, and hands to build durability in the tissue for heavy contact.

This product can be easily found at Asian markets, herb stores, ordered from a martial arts supplier, or made by anyone so inclined. Minimally it should be applied to and around the affected area until it dissipates into the skin then repeated.

Listed below are the herbs used in the Five Photo's Brand formula, but these can vary. It is strongest as an alcohol-based formula with the herbs combined and sealed in a 50+ proof rice-wine or vodka. Some brands add other herbs and/or remove some and, like wine, older is better.

Ingredients: Pu Huang (Cattail Pollen), Chi Shao (Red Peony), Dang Gui (Angelica Sinensis), Xue Jia (Dragons Blood), Ru Xiang (Frankincense), Mo Yao (Myrrh), Bo He (Peppermint), Hong Hua (Safflower), San Qi (Pseudoginseng Root).

Function: Moves Qi and Blood

Purpose: Used for centuries to heal bruises, contusions, sprains, and fractures, or for any tissue that can benefit from increased circulation. It also strengthens tissue in preparation for heavy contact by increasing blood flow and Qi to areas applied.

Application: Apply with the hands rubbing over the area of treatment. It is also effective using the wrap method described under "Castor Oil," just replace the oil with Dit Da Jow.

ZHENG GUI TUI NA (Tendon Lotion)

This product has properties like Dit Da Jow and is used to treat trauma damage to less vascular tissue (tendons and ligaments) and to build durability in advance to prevent injury.

ZHENG GU SHUI (Rectify the Bone or Bone Setting Solution)

This formula is over 500 years old and is used to treat arthritis, fractures, dislocations, sprains, and strains. About one-quarter of this herbal formulation is made from the powerful trauma injury herb "San Qi" also known as "Pseudoginseng."

PO SUM ON (Protect the Heart Oil)
This popular oil-based liniment with the funny name helps with circulation and contains warming cinnamon, but still has anti-inflammatory properties with cooling peppermint among its ingredients.

THAI OIL
Muay Thai fighters and trainers use this oil-based liniment extensively. Its oil-based quality allows it to stay on the skin surface longer where it traps in body warmth after being massaged onto the skin. This keeps the muscles warmer longer while bringing fresh blood to the area.

It has an unforgettable smell (not bad, just unforgettable) and as a side benefit for Muay Thai fighters it makes the body surface slippery making it difficult to hold, clinch, and apply direct penetrating contact.

SAN HUANG SAN (Three Yellow Powder)
This formula, also known as "Herbal Ice," is an ice replacement formula used for centuries by martial artists to treat traumatic injury. It has the unique quality of being able to reduce swelling while increasing local circulation to break up clotting and bruising. It is used primarily at the first stage of soft tissue and bone damage in place of ice.

It is a combination of 3 cold herbs that if taken internally clears what is known in Chinese Medicine as "damp heat" but applied externally it treats the swelling that results from traumatic injury.

There are plenty of commercial formulas available where versions of this can be purchased or it can be made by having equal quantities of the herb powdered at a Chinese herbal pharmacy, then mixing that with a base, such as Bees Wax or Vaseline, then stored and applied as needed.

Ingredients:
Huang Qin – Scutellaria – Skullcap Root
Huang Lian – Rhizoma Coptidis – Coptis Root
Huang Bai – Cortex Phellodendri – Phellodendron Bark
Zhi Zi – Fructis Gardenia Jasminoidis – Gardenia Fruit
Other Ingredients sometimes added:
Da Huang – Radix et Rhizoma Rhei – Rhubarb
Hong Hua oil – Flos Carthami – Safflower Oil

YUNNAN BAI (PAI) YAO (Stop Bleeding Powder)
This formula comes in powder or patch (External) or pill form (Internal) and is used to treat traumatic bleeding and to stop infection in open wounds. Asian warriors have used this for over a hundred years to help survive injuries sustained in battle. Its unique formulation stops bleeding while removing blood clots. The North Vietnamese used this formula extensively during the Vietnam War to help their soldiers survive and return to battle faster.

The powder is poured over the open wound then covered to stop bleeding, prevent infection, and speed up healing. It is also very useful in helping heal stitches and eliminate scarring.

Both powder and pill form also contain a tiny "red pill" for emergency oral use to treat any initial internal traumatic bleeding, infection, and to prevent shock, although these conditions should be treated professionally when help is available.

Note: Ground herbs in these raw formulas like San Huang San or Yunnan Bai Yao are mixed into a paste using a base that can range from saliva to water, egg whites, alcohol, lemon juice, vinegar, bees wax, Vaseline, etc.

DR. BOB'S MEDICINAL OIL
This modern *Po Sum On* formulation is a high potency blend of medicinal oils and Chinese herbs for relief of pain and inflammation in the musculoskeletal structure. It is available through Blue Poppy Herbs.

TEA TREE OIL
A powerful disinfectant for any skin infection, bug bite, scratch, etc.

The following are over the counter externally applied Sport Creams with recognizable names and are of 3 main types.

IODINE
This is a chemical element the body needs that it does not produce and especially beneficial for the thyroid. Iodine is also extremely useful to kill bacteria, viruses, fungi, and protozoa in the nasal passages. A watered-down version can be purchased over the counter that is put with a cotton swab into the nose to kill infections and prevent illness.

METHYL SALICYLATE CREAMS (Ben Gay, Tiger Balm, Icy Hot, etc.)
This is the Oil of Wintergreen family and a chemical cousin to aspirin. The commercial formulations generally also have Menthol and Camphor, which are not in the Salicylate or aspirin family.

These creams are used topically on intact skin for arthritis, back pain, sprains, strains, and bruises over select areas of the body. The menthol and camphor cools, or at least gives the sensation of coolness on the skin.

The chemical components are absorbed through the skin and into the bloodstream so repeated use over large parts of the body is not recommended. These should never be used over the entire body as this can be toxic, and they are contraindicated during pregnancy.

Note: The main Tiger Balm formulas come in red or white, with the red more warming and the white more cooling. The ancient Chinese formula that evolved into Tiger Balm is rumored to have contained Tiger bone. This may or may not be true, but the current formulation does not have it, and is not named for that reason.

TROLAMINE SALICYLATE CREAMS (Aspercreme, Myoflex, etc.)
This is a type of salt that is also a chemical cousin to aspirin but thought to be less toxic than Methyl Salicylate. It is used as a topical cream for muscle and joint pain to reduce swelling and inflammation.

CAPSAICIN CREAMS (Flexall, Icy Hot, Joint Flex, etc.)
This type of cream contains the main ingredient found in chili peppers and is commonly used for arthritis pain. It makes the skin feel hot and helps stop the pain sensation to the brain.

ICE
Ice is used to cool heat and reduce swelling. With an *acute injury* ice can and perhaps should be applied for up to 20 minutes. Common Western wisdom is to ice immediately then off and on for the next 48 hours. About 10 minutes on then at least 2 hours off. After the initial 48 hours, provided the injury is not severe, it is recommended to alternate between heat and ice for the next 48 hours.

Note: Ice is controversial in the holistic and TCM world where the belief is that it should not be used on traumatic injury because it inhibits the body's natural response to injury, which is swelling. Alternative methods to manage swelling are used without eliminating it by applying formulations like San Huang San and Dit Da Jow, that also help bring new healing blood, nutrients, and Qi to the area.

Precautions: The instant or disposable ice packs contain a chemical mixture that when mixed produces cold that is colder than the human skin can tolerate so they can burn the skin and leave scars. Put something between these instant ice packs and your skin. Real ice generally will melt before damaging the skin so is safer for direct contact use.

If something is already cold <u>do not</u> use ice.

HEAT
Heat loosens up cold stiff muscles and joints while making it easier for fresh blood, nutrients, and Qi to reach the tissue, all to speed up healing.

Dry heat (heating pads, fireplaces, room heaters) and moist heat (hot bath, steamed towel) methods are commonly used. Health practitioners have additional techniques and tools such as moxibustion and infrared heat lamps to direct heat in a more refined way.

Precaution: If something is already hot <u>do not</u> use heat.

BRACES-SUPPORTS-TAPING

This is a brief discussion of the importance of supporting and/or padding damaged or weak areas of the body. This is for anyone who exercises but especially for athletes actively training or competing.

Sports tape is the most flexible and popular item used by trainers everywhere. "Kinesio Taping" is a popular technique that can be seen on the internet. Enter "KT Tape" and the body part, or other sources exist. Cotton or neoprene braces are also recommended in many cases and often wrapped over with sports tape.

Expert advice is always recommended but at least research techniques used to protect different body areas. Here is a basic guideline for wrists, elbows, shoulders, low back, knees, and ankles.

<u>Wrists</u>: Tape and/or a brace should support around the joint line but is not applied too tightly as this could affect blood and nerve flow to the hand, especially through the carpal tunnel. The hand and forearm bones should also be connected by cross taping to increase overall reinforcement.

<u>Elbows</u>: Supporting the elbow is done with an appropriate brace or tape to hold the specific damaged tissue for support and to provide constant joint feedback. A support below the elbow joint (distal) at the forearms muscle tendons, or above the joint line (proximal) at the bicep/tricep tendons, or both sides tied together by crisscrossing, with the elbow bone exposed so movement can still take place.

Note: When the arm is not being used, or until it begins to feel better, wear a shoulder sling when possible. This relieves pressure by lifting the forearm and supporting the weight of the arm while immobilizing the elbow.

<u>Shoulders</u>: Supports for the shoulder are usually of the sling variety where the arm is incapacitated so the shoulder (and elbow) can rest. Taping can support a damaged shoulder for athletic use and is best done by someone trained in making a support mechanism from tape, or another specialized product, that allows for needed range of motion while protecting the structure as much as possible.

<u>Low Back</u>: Back supports are usually of the belt variety. The belt worn in traditional martial arts (Karate, Jiu Jitsu, Judo, etc.) not only holds the kimono together and shows rank level but its physical presence also and perhaps more importantly provides constant low back and abdominal support and core awareness. The traditional "drawstring" pants also add another layer of back support.

<u>Knees</u>: The four main knee injuries are Patellar Tendon strain (Patellar Tendonosis), ACL (Anterior Cruciate Ligament) strain or tear, MCL (Medial Collateral Ligament) strain or tear, and Medial Meniscus tear. See "Sprains & Strains for more details.

Patellar Tendon: This specialized brace is placed across that tendon below the knee to provide support. Common ailments needing this brace are "Osgood-Schlatter Disease" and "Runners Knee."

Anterior Cruciate Ligament (ACL): A slide-on cotton or neoprene knee support can give some feedback and early warning while providing a constant reminder as to having this injury.

Medial Collateral Ligament (MCL): This brace has solid (usually metal) hinges on both sides of the knee to inhibit lateral motion.
Medial Meniscus: Use the slide on cotton, neoprene, or patellar braces for some early warning, support, and a reminder of injury. Movement will still need to be modified, or it can be fixed surgically.

The severity of any knee injury determines whether tape and/or a brace would be enough to safely allow for hard training or competition.

Ankles: Use appropriate ankle support but best if also reinforced with tape at the attachments and weakest lines.

Summary Note: If in doubt seek expert advice. For practitioners of fighting arts some considerations for staying healthy include wearing required gear and perhaps additional protection, especially when training. These include mouthguard, groin protection, gloves, shin instep guards, headgear, or other protection that doesn't inhibit needed movement.

These assorted types of protection should be used by both participants to allow for longer more productive training sessions with less chance of injury. This is important at every level since we do not participate in these environments forever and we all want to be relatively healthy for the rest our lives after hard fighting days are over. Wear protection!

CUPPING & MOXIBUSTION
These very effective treatment methods are best done by someone trained in their application and use, primarily a Licensed Acupuncturist, although they can be done by a person on some of their own body areas.

INTERNAL TREATMENT METHODS
CHINESE HERBS
These are products from nature that can be used internally to treat different physical injuries. The single herbs listed here are used in TCM to treat characteristics of pain and numbness in the joints and muscles that result from over-training and/or physical injury.

These and others are most often used in formulas designed to treat specific conditions where they are ingested as teas or pills. This single herb list can provide some insight into this paradigm of healing but are most effectively and safely used as prescribed by an expert in Chinese Herbal Medicine or other knowledgeable practitioner.

Precaution: These herbs may not interact well with certain preexisting major health conditions or prescription medications. Use with caution!

DU HUO (Angelica Root)
Lower body pain, stiffness, weakness, low back, and leg cramping

QIANG HUO (Notopterygium Root)
Upper body pain and joint stiffness, mainly neck, shoulders, upper back

HAN FANG JI (Stephaniae Root)
Treats hot, red, swollen, painful joints

SANG ZHI (Mulberry Twig)
Treats swelling and edema in the joints

MU GUA (Quince Fruit)
Relaxes tight muscles and relieves muscle cramping

MO YAO (Myrrh Gum)
Treats internal illness, greatly benefits the skin, and reduces swelling

RU XIANG (Frankincense)
For traumatic injury, broken bones, sprains, and fractures, along with internal use when prescribed by a trained herbalist

SAN QI (Pseudoginseng)
Stops bleeding without causing clotting, reduces swelling, alleviates pain, and a main herb for traumatic injury (fractures, contusions, sprains, etc.)

NSAID's (Non-Steroidal Anti-Inflammatory Drug) & Acetaminophin
Drugs are sometimes needed, although they should be used in the most limited way possible. NSAID's and Acetaminophin are drugs used to treat pain, fever, and inflammation. Common over the counter NSAID's are *Ibuprofen, Acetylsalicylic Acid,* and *Naproxin,* with *Acetaminophen* in a separate category having other qualities.

Precaution: All NSAID's can cause stomach problems so they must be taken with food. What the drug reduces in the body (Prostaglandins) is also what protects the stomach lining, allowing ulcers and upper gastrointestinal bleeding to occur more easily from overuse.

IBUPROFEN (Motrin, Advil, etc.)
Anti-Inflammatory drug used to reduce swelling in damaged tissue. This can reduce the pain caused in oversized and swollen areas of the body. Unchecked swelling can cause pressure affecting the integrity of not only damaged tissue but surrounding tissue as well.

Purpose: When an injury first occurs, Ibuprofen is often recommended to keep initial swelling down so surrounding uninjured tissue is not impeded and/or damaged by the body's response to injury (swelling). This also allows the damaged tissue to be accessible for treatment. Many orthopedic doctors recommend up to 1000mg for several days in these cases.

Precautions: Many people take some form of Ibuprofen on an ongoing basis. One of the major problems with this, especially long-term, is it neutralizes the body's natural healing response to injury, which is swelling that brings new cells to the area and while eliminating old dead ones.

Taking Ibuprofen slows or eliminates this natural healing response by inhibiting new tissue formation. This means the tissue will never be able to fully heal as the fibroblast formation needed to replace the damaged tissue cannot take place while taking Ibuprofen.

The other major problem already mentioned is that these drugs are very hard on the stomach so at the very least should be taken with food to help protect the gut lining.

ACETYLSALICYLIC ACID (Aspirin: Bayer, Excedrin, etc.)
Aspirin is in the NSAID category but is unique and has a more long-term effect on the body chemistry. It is commonly recommended and used to thin the blood to help avoid the blood vessel blockage that can cause heart attacks and strokes.

Along with its popular blood thinning quality Aspirin is best used to treat dull, throbbing pain and fever, but is not as effective in treating cramps, bloating, or skin disorders.

Purpose: Thins the blood and reduces dull throbbing pain.

NAPROXEN (Aleve, Naprosyn, Midol, etc.)
Reduces the hormones that cause inflammation and body pain, so among other things women commonly use it to control menstrual cramping.

Purpose: Treats hormone related inflammation and pain.

Precaution: Naproxen can increase the risk of life-threatening heart and/or circulation problems, including heart attack or stroke.

ACETAMINOPHEN (Tylenol, etc.)
Without the anti-inflammatory effect of NSAID's, this works primarily in the brain to block pain messages and elevate the pain threshold.

Purpose: Relieves minor aches and pains such as headaches, muscle aches, back pain, toothache, and arthritis. It reduces fever and treats the aches and pains that accompany a cold.

Precaution: Overuse can cause Liver damage.

HOMEOPATHIC REMEDIES
This model of medicine was developed in Germany in the 1900's and is based on the "law of sameness" to treat sickness and injury. This means that taking minute trace elements of what is causing a health issue stimulates the body's natural healing response to that element.

Note: Most Western and Eastern health systems are based on the "law of opposites" so would treat hot conditions with cold, cold with hot, strengthen a weakness, reduce an excess, etc.

Homeopathy is akin to getting a flu shot or other vaccination where the disease is given to stimulate the body's natural resistance. However, Homeopathic doses are much smaller than any vaccination or flu shot.

These remedies are used to treat every manner of sickness and injury but are most effectively used when prescribed by a licensed practitioner after an extensive information intake. The main homeopathic remedy for trauma is Arnica Montana with a few others also listed.

ARNICA MONTANA
This homeopathic remedy can be found at most health food stores. It comes in pills for internal use and creams for external application (Arnica-Cream). It is useful for all trauma injuries especially bruises and inflammation. For trauma injury 30C is recommended. The formulations mostly are found in "X" and "C" strengths, with "C" the stronger dose.

Other Homeopathic Remedies to treat injuries include:
Calendula Officinalis - Promotes rapid healing
Bellis Perennis - Deep injury trauma plus sprains and bruises
Symphytum Officinale - Tendon injuries and fractures
Calcarea Phosphorica - Accelerates healing
Ruta Graveolens – Sore, aching, bruised bones, sprains
Rhus Toxicodendron - Sprains
Conium Maculatum - Contusions and bruises

RECOVERY THERAPY
Physical Therapy techniques are important when recovering from an injury, and to help prevent future injury. The three main categories are *Massage, Strength Building,* and *Stretching.*

These are best done under the guidance of educated professionals trained in various techniques. We can however do them to a lesser degree on ourselves, or with help from a caring layperson.

Note: A common treatment therapy uses the acronym R.I.C.E. meaning Rest, Ice, Compress, Elevate. Although easy to remember all components are not always relevant. *Rest* while *Elevating* are great ideas when time allows but *Ice* can be overdone as discussed earlier, and too much *Compression* can inhibit the flow of needed healing energy.

MASSAGE

Massage techniques are used to move tissue, blood, and Qi under the skin by stimulating areas on top of the skin. This type of treatment can be done on our self or by anyone with a mind to help whether trained or untrained in a formal massage technique, or by a paid professional. Massage techniques range from relaxing to more directed therapeutic treatments. Either should feel good, at least when it's over.

The relaxing variety helps us let go and feel happy where the therapeutic massage should feel achy and perhaps even painful, in a good way, as this is the sensation needed to break down scar tissue and move fresh blood and nutrients to the recovering tissue.

No sharp, nervy, or burning pain should ever be felt during a massage treatment. Any discomfort should be of the "hurt so good" type only. Do not get massage done on damaged or swollen tissue as this can cause further injury and delay the healing process.

Massage practitioners when working the whole-body are taught to massage towards the heart as this helps move the venous blood and lymph in the correct direction through the vessels. Specific area massage does not generally have this limitation as a muscle knot for example can and should be worked parallel and perpendicular to tissue fibers, and even while moving through ranges of motion.

Massage can be done dry, with oils, or lotions. Professionals formulate the major massage techniques into assorted styles or methods. There is every level of sophistication regarding massage but any of the following techniques can be used by anyone on anyone, including on our self. The key, as with all healing arts, is to do no harm.

Massage Techniques include: Squeezing/Grabbing; Rubbing/Stroking; Hitting/Patting; Twisting/Stretching; Pressing/Penetrating; and Rolling.

These methods are generally done with the hands and elbows but can also be done with the knees, feet, or with different tools such as in Gwa Sha where a scrapping instrument is used, or hot rocks, etc.

A massage tool from Chinese martial arts uses a solid heavy rod to roll over different body parts. This tool moves the qi in the tissue in a focused way by removing knots while stimulating in a way that strengthens muscles and tissue. This is commonly done on the forearms and shins.

A modern massage tool that uses a similar idea is the foam roller. It is lightweight and soft, so body weight can be used to sit or lay on it in a variety of ways, then moved so it can roll over/under tender areas with pressure. Areas rolled include the glutes, Iliotibial band, and back.

STRENGTH BUILDING

This important recovery step occurs mostly after an injury has healed. Since the muscles have been inactive they will have atrophied some from non-use. Start with natural body weight exercises then build up to adding weight, starting light then over time gradually increasing that weight.

Stabilizer muscle exercises that strengthen the support muscles of the body are often the starting point at this step of recovery, before moving to the larger specific use muscle groups. Get professional guidance and do your own research in this regard.

It is important in recovery and healing to challenge but not overwhelm the area affected. Get plenty of rest with good nutrition before the next treatment or session, and always listen to your body.

STRETCHING

Stretching is one of those methods that is easily done without professional guidance and is needed to fully recover from most injuries. Along with its many physical benefits stretching is also mentally and emotionally therapeutic.

It can be done when time allows almost anywhere to some degree, making it a convenient way to release stress without breaking a sweat or being in a workout environment. Yoga is a sophisticated system of stretching that is best learned with good instruction and not overdone, but minimally many of the movements can be researched and copied.

Stretching can be *Active* or *Passive,* as discussed in the Exercise Basics chapter, and there should never be sharp, burning, or nervy pain as stretching should feel good!

The lower back is a key area to keep stretched. My own low back issues after a car accident and observations of others prompted me to evolve the following routine over a 12-year period while teaching Tai Chi at my school. I regularly prescribe, demonstrate, and give a copy of it to anyone who presents to me with a low back problem. It cured my low back issue years ago and I have seen it help many people. Take it as my gift.

HEALTHY BACK STRETCHING ROUTINE

This routine, or any piece, can be done in bed in the morning or at any time on a comfortable floor surface. It usually takes 5-15 minutes but can take longer as moves can be held or repeated at a pace desired. These stretches can be done individually or in any order that feels good.

Start by lying flat on your back with your bent knees up
1. Hold front of your bent knees in each hand – begin circling your two knees in one direction while keeping your low back on the floor (head can be either flat or up). Repeat in other direction.

2. Hold one bent knee in both hands pulling it just outside of your chest while extending the opposite leg straight out, perhaps slightly off the ground. Feet can be flexed and extended as feels good. Repeat on opposite side.

3. Hold front of both bent knees in each hand then pull both knees towards your chest to gently lift your tailbone and hips off the floor, then release the knees so the muscles can engage as the hips fall. Repeat.

4. Place both feet flat on the floor with bent knees up and both arms out to the sides. Turn your face to one side and lay your knees to the opposite side onto that hip, trying to keep both shoulders flat on the ground. To increase the stretch grab and gently pull the top knee with your opposite hand moving it to where you feel the best stretch; straighten that top leg to add weight at the end of the stretch. Repeat on opposite side.

5. Hold front of bent knees in each hand then rock from side to side (left to right / right to left) allowing your low back to be massaged by the ground while using your elbows to push over to the other side. Repeat.

6. Starting with your knees in the air while lying flat on your back use your feet to kick-start (like on a swing at a playground) your body rolling forwards and backwards from tailbone to neck. Repeat.

Advanced: Sit up straightening your two legs in front reaching for your toes (fingers to toes) then roll back pulling your knees to your chest then over your head straightening your legs and arms to bring your feet towards the ground overhead reaching for your fingers (toes to fingers). Repeat.

7. Sit up with your two legs crossed in front while reaching forward with a straight back towards the wall in front of you (Superman style). Switch legs and repeat.

8. Turn over face down placing one bent leg in front under your hips and the other straight behind you. Repeat on opposite side.

9. Extend both legs behind face down with both hips on the ground and arms straight gently arching your back. Lift your hips sitting back onto your calves rounding your back while leaving your hands on the ground to stretch your shoulders. Repeat. Gently stand up when finished.

See Video Link at BarryBBarker.com

THE ART OF TEACHING MARTIAL ARTS

Why Teach? The best reason for teaching is to pass on the gift of martial arts to others, but first you must see it as a gift. As with any gift, it is not given with a desire for any special gratitude but for the sake of giving and how that will benefit the person receiving the gift. Teaching as a job for money is a factor, but time spent on the floor with student(s) should be the time when this gift is given.

People benefit from various aspects of martial arts to different degrees, but long time martial artists recognize the profound gift given to us. Students may not recognize or try to thank their teachers for this gift, although many will, but knowing that it has been a benefit to a student, at whatever level, is all the reward a true teacher needs.

Teachers also pass on information, so each generation doesn't have to reinvent what previous generations have already learned and discovered. The journey as a student cannot take place unless there are teachers willing and able to share their knowledge and experiences. Teachers were and are still students of their craft, so the benefits of giving reciprocate.

My experience with several martial art teachers is they all had a passion for what they teach. My Kenpo teachers were all dedicated and loyal followers of the art and style of Kenpo. Teachers from other martial arts I have studied were just as dedicated and passionate about their arts.

All the good teachers I have known not only knew their preferred style, but they infused a spirit into it that brought it to life. Most also respected the strengths of other styles while still being loyal to their own.

Really good teachers have a larger vision of their students, so they will teach them with the end in mind, and in a manner to benefit the youngest child to the oldest adult and everyone in between. The best teachers offer more than just good technique, but lessons in life while passing on knowledge and wisdom for the mind, body, and the spirit.

Teachers are not perfect people who always have noble intentions, but good teachers are dedicated practitioners of their craft who want to pass on that knowledge regardless of personal motivation. They also remain practitioners and students that seek knowledge when and where possible. This enthusiasm, dedication, and passion for a craft can be contagious and seems to exist in successful teachers.

Being able to know the benefits gained by teaching over an extended period I am grateful for enthusiastic students who are anxious to learn. Whether learning something new or improving upon something old a teacher is rewarded by students who appreciate the benefits of their teaching efforts.

This chapter is for those who teach, plan on teaching, or end up teaching. Since teaching is part of learning, teachers everywhere require it of their higher-level students. With my students, this begins at the advanced or Brown Belt level of training. After all, knowledge and insight are relative, as all good teachers know.

How to Teach Martial Arts
Many have heard of, or experienced, a teaching method that uses *negative reinforcement* where punishment, pain, and often insult is directed at those not performing well to generate discipline, focus, and effort.

The roots of this are probably in the military where techniques like these have been used in boot camps over the millennium and around the world. This method may or may not be necessary when preparing for war, but it does not work well outside of the military in places like commercial martial arts schools with children, teens, and civilian men and women.

The better approach for these non-military personnel is *positive reinforcement*. This is when good effort and improvement are noticed, pointed out, recognized, and reinforced. This causes more effort and improvement and has the side benefit of making anyone not working hard try harder to get some of that recognition, which they should then get.

Even though curriculum is important the primary goal of a teacher is to teach students how to think, analyze, and understand for themselves. An old saying describes this gift the teacher has the power to give. *"If you give a man to fish you feed him for a day, if you teach him how to fish, you feed him for a lifetime."*

When a student becomes *self-corrective* because their understanding of what they have been taught is thorough, then you can consider yourself a good and successful teacher. Educate, don't indoctrinate.

It is also important to a martial arts business that students enjoy your classes, which should be safe, fun, educational, require effort, and be rewarding. Children must be kept under control with teens and adults focused, but classes should be an enjoyable activity that a student looks forward to attending.

When class is over kids should leave remembering how fun and empowering it was, where teens should feel increased confidence and perhaps have enjoyed the social environment. Adults want to discover, gain new awareness, and understand what they are learning, so they should leave with some new insight(s), all after a good workout. Everyone should have been treated with respect and felt the time was well spent.

Workouts should be physically exhausting and mentally challenging, and at no time should anyone get hurt due to negligence, or ever feel intimidated. In all cases it must be enjoyable and rewarding.

A good teacher is focused with a mind for the learning environment and to the mix of students, so everyone can benefit from the class. When pairing off put students together who seem to relate to each other and can work together. This can be done by sex, age, size, aggressiveness, passiveness, etc. Watch everyone, but especially anyone dangerous to work with as they will lose you students.

Martial arts are for everyone, especially the weak and the timid. Take care of them so they will not quit before they can gain the benefits of training. Put the rough, tough people together and let them bang on each other so long as their emotions remain calm and they are not injuring one another, while also having a positive experience.

For children, FUN and REWARD are the keys because they must look forward to coming to your class, or you will not have a class. You must however keep control as they must behave and be respectful while in your facility. Children need this valuable life skill, and it is possibly a main reason their parents enrolled them.

A standard children's group class should consist of an exercise period, a curriculum period, and a play/fun period. The amount of time on each can vary depending on any special focus of the school at that time (testing, upcoming tournament, demo, etc.).

It is also important to have a reward system in place where students, especially kids, can earn stripes on their belts, a new color of belt, and other bonuses for their efforts. Everyone enjoys the recognition given them in these circumstances so be sure to acknowledge them to the group, who should then clap to applaud their accomplishment.

These moments are extremely beneficial to motivation, attendance, and long-term retention. This then leads to all the many lifelong benefits. Other methods like good behavior recognition in the form of a sticker at the end of class for kids that accumulate towards a cool prize, or even a hand stamp is important. Adults and teens are also motivated by stripes and belts, but also must enjoy the workouts and social environment, with everyone requiring some variety in the training.

This variety can be created on the spot based upon class dynamic and whatever the theme of the day/week is, but if after a long day or week of teaching the creative juices are not flowing then having a list of ideas can be helpful. Attached is a "Group Class Cheat Sheet" for instructors from my karate floor of warm-ups, exercises, drills, and games that can be used for different ages, levels, and size of classes.

GROUP CLASS CHEAT SHEET

WORKOUT FORMATS
Line Drills; In Place
Row(s); Moving Row(s)
Circle(s) / Partner(s)
Circuit Training
Follow the Black Belt
Follow the Student
Ball Skills *(Bounce, Lob,
Bowl, Hike, Under / Over
Pitch, Volleyball,etc.)*
Jungle Walk (kids)
Herding Cats (kids)

PARTNER EXERCISES
Team Fitness *(Strength,
Endurance, Flexibility)*
Partner Stretching
Wheel Barrow
(Walking/Pushups)
Piggy-Back *(Ride/Squats)*
Plow; Leap Frog

STRETCHING
Passive Movement
(All Joints ROM)
Passive & Dynamic
Stretching
*(Chinese Splits, Front to
Back Splits, Butterfly,
Reverse Butterfly, etc)*
Partner Stretching
Leg Swings *(Front, Back,
Side, Circle In/Out)*

CONTACT DRILLS
Bag & Pad Work
*(Heavy Bag, Shield,
Paddle, Hand Mitts,
Beach Ball-Kids)*
Blocking Drills
(Inside Down/Out/Down)
Self-Def Techniques
*(Partner, Line, Gauntlet,
Monkey in Middle)*
Sparring *(Freestyle,
Point, Boxing, KB, Clinch,
MMA, Takedown, Position
& Submission Grappling,
Wing It, Shoulder / Hip /
Knee Tap, Push Hands)*
Stomach Punches
Leg Kicks *(Inside & Out)*
Shoulder Hits

CARDIO EXERCISES
Running *(jog, sprint,
intervals,knees up, heels up)*
Jumping Jacks *(Reg, Rev,
Seal, Diag w/ wo punches)*
1 or 2 Foot Hop/Jump
Skipping *(height/distance)*
Horse Gallup *(Side Shuffle)*
Front/Rear Crossovers
(Grapevine Step)
Crab Walks
Snail Crawls
(Moving Recover Position)
Crawls*(Bear, Army,
Zombie, Caterpillar)*
Monkey Runs
Rabbit Runs
Mummy Walks
Frog Jumps
Duck Walks
Hip Escape / Shrimping
(Alternating, One-Side)
Use Floor Dots *(jump over
front/back, side/side,
cover/see, etc.)*
Burpees *(w/ wo pushup)*

BASICS
Footwork
Switches; Step Drag;
Step-Thru; Drag Step;
Front/Rear Crossover;
Combo Footwork

Kicks
Any In-Place
Any with Footwork
Any on Targets

Block/Punch/Strike
Individually In-Air
In Combination
On Targets w/Partner(s)

Combos & Counting
Build a Combo (Team)
Roll the Dice
Playing Cards
Pyramid

Falls/Rolls/Ground
Maneuvers

CARDIO EXERCISES
Gymnastics
*(Shoulder or Barrel Rolling,
Cartwheels, Walk on
Hands, Frogstand,
Head/Handstand, etc.)*
Strength
*(Push-ups, Sit-ups, Pull-
ups, Dynamic Tension)*
Squats
*(In-Place, Lunges, Jumps,
Chinese Chairs)*
Knee to Feet Jump-ups

LADDER DRILLS
Forward & Sideways
1-2-3 feet each square
Jumping Jacks
Left-Right Slide
*(2 In 1 out; 2 In 2 Out
1 In 2 Out Rear Cross, etc)*
2-feet: Downhill Ski, etc
Front/Rear Crossover
In/Out R-L or L-R
Scissor *(Ali shuffle)*
Sparring Bounce
Fish Tail

GAMES
Dodge Ball
Cream the Kids
Simon Says *("Mr/s Says")*
Noodle Game/Fighting
Lord of the Ring
Tug-of-War
Black Belt / White Belt
(Red Light / Green Light)
Tag *(Freeze, etc.)*
Hot Potato
Musical chairs
3-Legged Race
Dizzy Izzy
Roll the Dice
Duck-Duck Goose
Olympics
*(Arm Wrestling, Forearm
Wrestling, Leg Wrestling,
Hand Slap, Thumb War,
Rock/Paper/Scissor, etc)*
Modified Team Sports
*(Baseball, Kickball,
Basketball, Soccer)*

What to Teach

The goal is to teach meaningful and valuable curriculum while passing on life lessons from which students can benefit on many levels. A martial arts teacher gives students the opportunity to not only exercise and learn self-protection but can calm an aggressive ego or build a weak one.

This helps eliminate daily insecurities and fears that can lead to being bullied or being a bully. Bully's intimidate and prey on the weak and those lacking in confidence at every age, stage, and status of life. Having the confidence that accompanies martial arts skill humbles and trains people allowing them to relax and live happy, healthy, more productive lives.

The best teachers are also not afraid of giving away their knowledge to worthy students. Not all at once as students need time to absorb and be deserving, but your knowledge must be taught to someone or it will be wasted. This is the one selfish reason for teaching that an old Chinese saying puts well, *"If you give it, you keep it; if you keep it, you lose it."* Your gift must be shared, or it is no longer a gift.

You should also not be afraid that one of your students might outgrow the need for you as their instructor someday or become physically better than you in one or more aspects of their training. Remember the only constant in life is change. People learn, grow, and improve so a student could learn everything you have to teach them.

It's a good reflection on you if your students are intelligent, independent thinkers who can function on their own. Besides, current and past students of good teachers always speak favorably of them. Without your skill and selflessness giving keys to knowledge they would not have unlocked all the doors to success they have.

Even if some don't realize it at the time they will eventually so rest easy and feel proud of their success, which reflects your success. This is also reason for teachers to continue growing so they always have something new to teach students. Since eventually we all grow older, relying on athleticism and fighting prowess must be gradually replaced by wisdom and experience, so keep learning.

Teaching vs. Business

Always keep these two separate. If you are responsible for the business, then this should be done in the designated office or business area. Teaching should be done in the training area, so DO NOT do or talk business in the training area, or train in the business area.

When you and your students enter the training area you and they are on a formal basis with a goal of practicing and learning martial arts. If they want to talk with you about payments or terms or something not martial arts related, then take them to the designated business area or refer them to the appropriate person off the training floor.

If someone wants to "BS" with you then take that out of the training area as well. It may not seem like a big deal at the time, but it adds up to a lack of respect for the training area, and informality with the teacher in that environment. This can evolve into diminished respect and casualness, with the training area losing some of its unique and special quality.

How to Treat Students
It's not about you!!! This is the student's time to learn and grow. Students should be treated with respect and taught at a pace where they can learn and absorb. If a student does not understand something the teacher is at fault. Change your explanation or slow down and be happy with smaller successes.

From my experience, the order most teen and adult students learn is Mind, then Body, then Spirit. When teaching a teen or adult it is useful to give an intellectual understanding while showing the movement. Then guide them into developing a mind/body connection into muscle memory. They should see, feel, and understand (Mind), then do the movement (Body) before infusing more enthusiasm and commitment (Spirit).

Kids, from my experience, learn Body first, then Spirit, followed by Mind. With children, it is better to put their bodies in motion to develop coordination and muscle memory first (Body). Then inspire their imaginations to move with enthusiasm while having fun (Spirit). The intellectual understanding (Mind) evolves more slowly with most kids, as it is boring and often unintelligible. All of this however can and should be customized to fit different students.

How to Teach
Be friendly, know student's names and say their name when teaching them. Remember the 4 E's of teaching: Energy, Example, Enthusiasm, and Excellence. This helps make teaching and learning a positive experience.

People learn in three major ways that relate directly to the mind-body-spirit concept. Those are Auditory (hear it explained) opening the Mind to additional information, Kinesthetic (feel/do it) engaging the Body to action, and Visual (see it with the eyes) to infuse the Spirit with enthusiasm.

Everybody uses these to some degree with the goal to strive for balance, so learning can be most effective. Different people may tend to favor one method more than another, so an observant instructor will use this observation to help each student learn in the best way for them.

The Auditory learners are the thinkers, needing analogies, metaphors, and an intellectual understanding to help their minds process the reasons for moving in this way. An intellectual understanding would include explaining Ideas, Theories, Concepts, and Principles, along with providing reasons for wanting to know this information. Appealing to these thinkers through their minds will intrigue them.

The Kinesthetic people need to feel the effectiveness of a technique, with control of course, but the "wow" effect is powerful to them. They need to touch and be touched to relate to the instruction and the information. Even patterns done "in the air" like Sets & Forms will be absorbed better when bodywork is included for these types especially.

The Visual people need to see a demonstration of what you want them to learn so they have a picture in their mind. The teacher must direct and train a student's eyes where and what to look at while they are watching the teacher or someone else demonstrating a skill.

In a group class environment, all three methods should be used so everyone is engaged and learning. The goal for a teacher should be to help students improve perception in each of the auditory/mind, kinesthetic/body and visual/spirit areas.

Additional bullet points for teachers:

Teaching Environment Goals

Where students learn is important and should be safe, clean and free from hazards. Each class should have these four things as goals.
1) Every student gets a great workout
2) Every student learns something new or gets better at something old
3) Everyone has fun, is treated with respect, and gets deserved praise
4) Every effort is made to avoid injuries

Safety and First Aid
1) Look for hazards in the environment then fix or report it
2) Be aware of everyone's safety always while training
3) Students must wear appropriate safety equipment
4) Prevention: Never assume a student understands your instructions
   (Note: Beginner's / White Belts are the most dangerous people)
5) If someone gets hurt sit him or her out and assess the injury
   (See "First Aid" section for useful information in this regard)
6) In case of injury report to whoever is responsible for the facility

The Order of Teaching Physical Curriculum
1) Mechanics / Form / Detail / Knowledge *(teach by the numbers)*
2) Power / Leverage / Angle / Effectiveness / Intent / Purpose
3) Timing / Flow / Relaxation
   "The mind is the presence of intention, the eyes are the focus of intention, movement is the action of intention, and breath is the flow of intention."
4) Speed / Explosiveness / Acceleration / Quickness / Hustle / Effort
5) Options / Combinations / "What ifs?" / Creativity / Natural Strengths
6) Tricks / Hidden Moves / Subtleties / Insight

Tips for Teachers
1) Children are people to so don't treat them like babies. Speak normal with age level vocabulary. Give everyone respect and never be condescending.

2) Don't bend over and speak down to kids or shorter people. Squat or sit as needed to give perspective for teaching, and to save your back
3) Be animated & motivated
4) Simplify your commands
5) Detect & correct errors ASAP, but don't drive students crazy
6) Provide extra insight & variations for faster learning students
7) Provide positive feedback *(positive reinforcement for kids especially)*
8) Be innovative & creative

Before Group Classes
1) Help with attire and begin organizing students for class while being friendly and engaging *(straighten uniforms, fix belts, handwraps, etc.)*
2) Politely remind about rules as necessary *(no jewelry, gum chewing, shoes, don't lean on the walls or mirrors, etc.)*
3) Make new students feel welcome and comfortable by knowing their name and introducing them to at least one other friendly student
4) Assign a buddy to a new student for the first class, especially kids
5) Line students up at the scheduled start time in seniority order with higher students closer to the front

During Group Classes
1) See "Group Class Cheat Sheet" for ideas on ways to warm up and work out a class besides the regular curriculum and sparring
2) Learn all the student's names
3) Encourage, push, and motivate students to work hard and not quit
4) Keep order in class and everyone busy – no standing around or BS'ing
5) Do not talk too much - avoid lecturing and never talk down to anyone
6) Help students to save face if/when something embarrassing happens
7) Have a plan for class. Don't stand and watch, stay active
8) Be aware of everyone all the time
9) Show off occasionally but only in glimpses - pick your moments

After Group Classes
1) Have students line up
2) Award any stripes, belts, certificates, or note any special recognition
3) Verbally review lessons or themes and ask for questions
4) Say something about future training and make any announcements
5) Introduce & thank any new students or guests in attendance
6) Conclude and finish (bow out)
7) Shake everyone's hand in rank order and have them shake each other's
8) Say their names with words of encouragement while shaking hands
9) Check on individual students that are new or anyone who may have had an issue during class *(injuries, close calls, loss of temper, funny moments, embarrassing moments, etc.)*
10) Put stuff away
11) Make notes of lessons you learned or discussions for other instructors

How to Teach Private Lessons
1) For a New Student

a) Greet in lobby
b) Get student ready for class *(shoes off, bow into area, etc.)*
c) Bring them to the lesson area, put in position
d) Politely explain rules and formalities *(keep it light)*
e) Formally start class *(bow-in, "let's begin", etc.)*
f) Start by teaching Beginning Level Curriculum
g) Review about 5 minutes before the end of their scheduled time
h) With kids do something fun then end on time
i) If a child, speak with parent(s) about the lesson *(stay positive)*
2) For a Current Student
a) Greet and take to lesson area
b) Improve something old and/or add something new
c) Start review 5 minutes before lesson time ends
d) End on time - others may be waiting

Note: As kids grow, their bodies become longer so their stance width when they were 7 is not the same as when they are 14, among other things. An instructor needs to keep adjusting a student's structure, body awareness, movement, power, and control to reflect the length and strength of their body as they grow and develop.

THE BUSINESS OF MARTIAL ARTS

I included this chapter for anyone interested in being in the martial arts business. This is not for most people, but I wanted to share my insights with anyone currently or considering doing this for a living. Many of my insights apply to other types of businesses as well.

Being a martial arts school owner for me has been a blessing, so if you are considering being in my field then read on, otherwise skip this section.

So, you do want to be a Martial Arts School Owner? Do you really want to earn your livelihood as a martial arts instructor? Do you really want to be your own boss, set your own hours, make your own decisions, help your fellow man, and make a lot of money? Wow, where do I apply for that job? Does that sound too good to be true? It may be! Running your own business is demanding work that requires your time and dedication over a long time for you to be considered successful at it.

Telling people that you're a martial arts instructor does not impress as many people as you might think. Oh, they may think that you could beat them up, but they won't think of you like they would a doctor, scientist, astronaut, or firefighter. If you're looking for instant prestige from your position, think again. It takes a long time to build credibility and even then, when you meet someone new you start all over again.

You can't let the prestige your student's give you go to your head. Black Belts are a dime a dozen in modern times as everyone seems to know someone who is a "Black Belt," and often they are young children. There will also be enough 35-year old Grandmasters around to keep you from taking yourself too seriously. Stay humble.

What about this notion of setting your own hours, being your own boss, making your own decisions? I can tell you from personal experience this is highly overrated. For example, if you decided you wanted to open your school at midnight and close at 6:00am you would discover quickly you don't have the power you thought, considering you're the boss.

A business is dependent on customers being able to attend, so in the martial arts business the hours must reflect the free time of your students. You will not watch prime time TV while running a martial arts school and your family should also be involved since you will not spend much time at home having a "normal life" until maybe Sunday, unless there's a tournament or event. Get the idea.

What if you decided you don't like children because hey, you're the boss and you don't like the little #*!?@^ so you refuse to teach them. What if you want to be irritated and scary to the children, teens, or adults you do teach because you're the boss? Sorry, it doesn't work that way. You can be mean and grumpy, but you won't have many (if any) students.

You must be nice and pleasant every time and all the time with the public. So, if you think you are going to be the boss think again. The customer has the power. You are their servant!

Maybe you want to have tough students, so you beat them up and they beat each other up whenever they come to class. The joke goes that you will achieve your goal and have the two toughest students in town. The irony is that students who survive in this type of school probably didn't need self-defense training to begin with as nobody was messing with them in real life.

The people who need the skills you teach the most are the fearful, weak, and insecure. Students will become tougher over time, but it is not something you can force on them if you want to have students.

What about that dream of helping your fellow man to develop them self as people. Even if you are the wisest and most honorable martial artist of all time you may not have the impact on as many students as you wish.

Realistically you will only see most students a few hours each week and most will not be around longer than a year or two, with a small percentage reaching a Black Belt level. Most will not spend enough time for you to have the major effect you envision.

Does this mean you shouldn't try your best? Of course not, you must give each student your best because it is the right thing to do. Teachers must not be disappointed if a student does not stay long enough or recognize or acknowledge what is being given them. Remain committed. It will come back to you in time from a few that make it all worthwhile.

If your heart is in the right place of wanting the best for every student, then give them the best you have. It will most likely not be your fault when some people quit as this happens for many reasons including money, moving, attainment of initial goals, other interests, schedule changes, etc.

Don't take it personally. Wish them well and send them on their way feeling good about you and your school. They may be back someday, or bring, or send others, but at the least they will speak favorably of you and your program.

Want to make a lot of money? Sure, doesn't everybody? The term "a lot of money" is relative however. The potential exists to make a comfortable living running a martial arts school, but you will not make the millions you dream of running one full-time school, although there are chain schools that can make these "big bucks."

However, if living a relatively comfortable life is enough then yes, you can make a lot of money running a successful martial arts school. If you want millions then probably no, you cannot make a lot of money. You need to determine for yourself if the time is worth the reward.

I don't mean to sound negative about being a professional martial artist, but I want you to realize it will never be easy. It requires your time, energy, creativity, patience, consistency, and your common sense to run a successful martial arts business. If you're looking for an easy and glamorous job this is not it.

Now that I've played devil's advocate and given some negatives, do you still want to earn a living as a martial arts instructor? I hope you do because for me, I love this job! I had spent a couple years in the restaurant business as a teenager then a dozen years in manufacturing before running my martial arts school. For me this is the most rewarding job I have ever done, and I would not trade it.

It suits my personality, my interests, my lifestyle, and my being. If this is what you want to do, then open your eyes to the reality and go for it. First and foremost, keep training and watch what other successful school owners do while asking questions, making mental and physical notes, then at some level of training you may have your opportunity.

Here are some tangibles and intangibles I have learned while running a successful martial arts school for 30+ years as of this writing. This is not a business manual, but it is insight based upon my experience that I hope can help your school or club grow and be successful.

GOALS
Long Term = 10 Years; Medium Term = 5 Years; Short Term = 1 Year
Writing out these personal and business goals is a very useful effort that I have done twice to date, once when I was 25 then again when I was 40. In both cases I was able to achieve and surpass those goals but writing them down proved to be very powerful.

LONG TERM GOALS: To make the commitment necessary to run a full-time martial arts school you must decide if you are willing to spend the time to become established in your community. If the answer is no, get a regular job. If yes, then plan your personal life around your school.

You should live in the area, your children (if applicable) should attend the local schools and you should shop locally, etc. Talk this decision over with those who will be affected by it, do some soul searching and become 100% committed. Do not do this halfway!

Also determine if you are the type of person who can make it in this business. Running a martial arts school is a service oriented and personality driven business so you need to genuinely like people, and people need to like you.

You will meet many types of people, many who you will bond with instantly, and others that grow on you in time, and some you would not normally associate with or maybe even like. However, eventually you learn to appreciate all your students regardless of personal chemistry.

A harsh reality in life, and especially in business, is that you must be pleasant and polite all the time with customers and students. There are many times when you must be bigger than the irritated and irritating people around you.

It is often difficult but we all must "suffer the fools" sometimes and that is especially important in business. Besides, everyone has bad days, so a non-judgmental and unoffended attitude is necessary as sometimes we just catch someone at a stressful moment or time in his or her life.

It should be mentioned that the money in the traditional martial arts business is in teaching children. Many parents recognize the life skill benefits associated with martial arts for children. If you do not like or cannot teach children, then do not plan on having a large traditional type school.

It is true that you can teach only adults by offering a hybrid or a specialized adult style, and/or martial arts fitness and make a decent living. The perception of "adult curriculum" changes with time and culture so Karate classes in an earlier time had mostly adult students, before sport fighting gyms became popular. Since change is the only constant nobody knows what the future holds.

The most important aspect in teaching martial arts is that you are providing a service to the public. If you are a loner who doesn't like people, then don't get into this profession. If you are enthusiastic about life and like to share that enthusiasm with your fellow man, then go for it.

MEDIUM TERM GOALS: With your 10-year commitment fully digested and understood determine where you want to open a facility, then plan student development, and money making strategies. As cold as it may sound, making money is the top priority because if you don't make money then neither you nor your students will have a place to train and learn.

Before committing to a full-time school, it may be wise to start a small club or community program and see if you can build it. If successful decide if you want to develop that into a larger school, then begin working on the time frame for expansion. Determine how many students you will need before expanding while organizing and writing down your thoughts.

It is your responsibility to run a reputable school so do not open one if you have any doubt about succeeding. All your future students will be relying on you to stay in business, so they can have a long-term facility to attend. Do not add to the bad rep so many deadbeat martial arts instructors have left in the wake of their business failures. Be a good and responsible businessperson.

Once you have picked a community that is right for your new business then you need to find a location, negotiate a lease, perhaps get a loan, then build out and set up your facility. There is a lot to do and it never ends. If you are up for it then remember that in business, you usually need to spend money to make money. If you're feeling confident, read on!

SHORT TERM GOALS: Once the "what" "where" "when" "how" and "why" to open your martial arts school is determined then it's time to get down to business. Sit down with a pencil and big note pad to plan your first year. Dream a little and write out your wish list. Temper it with reality later.

What's the name of your business? Do you have a logo? What are your marketing strategies? When are you going to open? When are your presales going to start? What will be your business hours and group class schedule? What are the demographics in your area? Who will be your students? Where could you do demos or presentations (elementary schools, churches, clubs, etc.) and check with the local Chamber of Commerce for a list of community events and activities that you could become involved with for some networking opportunities.

Find out about local tournaments where you can make your presence felt. Plan, or at least leave room, to evolve some events throughout the year. These can vary from a student Photo Day, Women's Free Self-Defense Classes, Belt Testing, Awards Night, In-School Tournaments, Holiday Parties, Sales, etc. Leave flexibility but make a general plan of events and spread them throughout the year.

OVERALL ANALYSIS:
If you have determined at this point this is the business for you, and you have a general idea of what you would like to accomplish your first year in business, first 5 years in business, first 10 years, then it's time to get down to business and open a facility. The fun is just beginning.

SCHOOL PHILOSOPHY
Start with what you envision but in time your school will develop a personality of its own, although your attitude goes a long way in determining that personality. You can't go wrong following the Golden Rule, aka Matthew 7:12, which says "Do unto others as you would have them do unto you." This applies to your life and to you at your school so treat others the way you would like to be treated. Here's a few guidelines:

1) Always give people the benefit of any doubt and be more than fair
2) Never lose your temper in public
3) Accept many eyes see you as a role model and look to you for guidance
4) Be professional always in your business
5) Leave some martial arts mystique for your students to ponder
6) Be family oriented and appreciative of the good you are doing for your students and the community.

7) Say "hello" and "goodbye" with a smile, a wave and/or a handshake to everyone you can as they enter and leave your facility (think of them as welcome visitors to your home and treat them as such).

BUSINESS PHILOSOPHY
It is important that you develop and maintain good business habits. Here are some suggestions.

Business Attitude
Running a martial arts school is a personality driven business so have a personality, but still be professional. Be friendly and fun but what you say and do is being observed so avoid discussions or polarizing topics (like politics and religion). Everyone has the right to their own views and beliefs and your business is not the place to discuss social issues that may stir emotions and make people uncomfortable or not like you.

Respect everyone and don't judge anyone's ability to pay for your services by what they look like. Give everyone you speak with the benefit of any doubt as long as you don't feel physically threatened and your business atmosphere is not being compromised. Always be polite and courteous while presenting your business in the best way to anyone interested.

Watch your language. Don't use anything close to profanity or inappropriate innuendos near students, their family members, or others, especially inside your business, as you cannot know what might offend someone.

Remember that business is business, so all are welcome who do not take away from other students and their families enjoying your facility.

Do Your Paperwork/Computerwork
It is critically important that you complete any daily, weekly, and monthly paperwork. It can be tedious, but <u>it must be done</u>. Don't get lazy regarding this important part of managing your business.

Business Security
Although it is important that you are polite and respectful while giving current and potential customers the benefit of any doubt, you must also not be foolish with business information. In other words, don't give away more than is necessary to make the sale or conclude a conversation.

People may want to know how you do it. Explain in generalities. "I put in a lot of hours," or "It's easy when you have a good product," or "I'm fortunate to be in such a supportive community," etc. Questions may be innocent enough but keeping answers general works best.

Shred papers with information about your business. This includes student lists, forms, or any information that could help anyone understand how you run your business, or from criminals getting anyone's personal or financial information. Spying on competitors is very common in business so what better place to find information than in their trash can.

There are also those who will call trying to gain more than the normal information, perhaps pretending to be a potential customer. Cyber security is another important consideration in modern times so take necessary precautions to try and protect your business.

Competitors may want to know about you and you may want to know about them. For me I never worried about the competitors as I was always more focused on running my own business to the best of my abilities, so the competition would worry about me.

I suspect that I have gotten phone calls from competitors disguising their true intentions to ask for information about prices and programs. It can be difficult to tell so I never worried about it and just followed my general sales presentation with everyone, never being shy about saying general price information or talking about programs. I figured if my competition was that worried about me then I was already winning.

Some general rules for phone inquiries: Don't get into long drawn out conversations with people that you don't know because 1) You don't have time; 2) It's not good business; 3) Potential students don't often pay you over the phone: 4) Potential students cannot take a lesson over the phone. They must come in or they are just looky-loos, so get to the point of when they can come in to see your facility and don't waste too much time.

SALES PHILOSOPHY
Be Fare - Be Responsible - Be Honest
Having a sales philosophy is highly recommended. The options are either present a product worth more than you can possibly charge for it or try to "rip people off." It is far better for many reasons and on many levels to pick the first option. This should be a no-brainer.

Conmen exist in every field, including martial arts. They can rip people off for a time, but this philosophy inevitably catches up to them resulting in business failure. They also lose much, if not all the trust and respect the students, their families, and other people in the community have given them.

This lack of responsibility not only affects them, but it damages the martial arts industry where most of us strive to build and maintain the integrity of that industry. Be responsible. Do the right thing all the time.

I recommend charging less than your service is perceived to be worth, with that perception the key to every sale. Make the perception (and hopefully the reality) of your service as worth much more than you could possibly charge for it. This is good business, and at the essence of good sales. Be fare yet competitive when setting your rates but your presentation determines the perceived value.

As Black Belts we know what the martial arts have done for us and how much we want others to benefit the way we have. This makes what we have to offer priceless to us. That needs to be conveyed to a prospective student (or their parents) in a way that when they do see the price they will be relieved that the cost is much less than their perception of gain.

Some in the public perceive martial arts training like other activities such as baseball, soccer, dancing, gymnastics, football, weight training, or aerobics classes. A full appreciation of our passion, and how unique and special it is, may not be completely understood by them in an interview, or through a trial or introductory program. So long as they start classes we must believe that those benefits will manifest over time.

Be enthusiastic about what you have to offer because, in business especially, *you are as you are perceived, not as you perceive*. Be honest and relate stories of success and/or your own story, but don't over sell the service or promise specific benefits. Offer the potential for learning, training, and growing at your school.

How to Think When People Inquire About Lessons
Always presume that inquiring people are already sold on the idea of lessons. Remember, you did not make them call, or go get them and make them come into your facility. Learn to deal with objections (Sales 101) and leave it to up to them to say if they are not interested.

Your predetermined perception that they are already sold eliminates any hesitation you may have about them. This enables you to control the conversation and help guide them through the interview process and eventually into classes.

If after a professional sales presentation that eliminates obstacles and helps guide a prospective student, they do not commit to taking lessons don't worry about it. You did the best you could so get basic information and thank them for coming in and end the conversation gracefully.

You can follow up with them later or they may come back in the future, but at the very least they should feel good about the time at your facility and their interaction with you, and they may refer others even if it wasn't for them at that time.

Don't take sales rejection personally. If you did something wrong and you know it all you can do is correct the problem, so it doesn't happen again.

How to Act When People Inquire About Lessons
It generally takes a certain amount of courage for a layperson to walk into a martial arts facility and inquire about lessons. Give them the benefit of the doubt and make it as easy and comfortable as possible. Smile even though they may seem tense or nervous. Show them you are a regular person and that you have a service to offer that has many benefits for them and/or their children.

Although it is important to be friendly and make people feel comfortable you must also stay on task since you generally will not have time to "chat." Interview the potential student and give them some options. Either they will be starting on a certain date, or you will be following up with them on a certain date, or they are not interested. In any case, you control the conversation and lead them to decide.

The Keys to the Sale
1) Be sold on the service or product you are selling.
2) Make a good presentation by guiding a potential student through the process while maintaining control of the conversation.
3) Do everything for new students except write their check, etc.
4) Don't be afraid to ask for the money. "How would you like to pay, Cash, Check, or Charge?" Your time and expertise are worth more than you could charge for it so don't be afraid to ask for payment.
5) Smile, have a good time and enjoy life. Don't be grumpy or get uptight with people. Remember that saying "happiness is a manner of traveling and not a destination" or the "Ice Ball Theory" that in a billion years the sun will burn out and nothing anybody who ever lived, said, did, or thought will matter. Don't take yourself too seriously!

20 Tips to Help You Stay in Business

1. **Show up on-time, every time.** *(There is No Excuse for being late!)*

2. **Keep your business and yourself clean and looking professional.**

3. **Martial Arts instruction is a personality driven service business.** *(People must like you. Be serious when doing your job but otherwise smile, be personable, easy to talk to, non-judgmental, and friendly. Remember: It's about how you make people feel that counts!)*

4. **Treat customers in your business like welcome visitors to your home.** *(Be glad they have come and if possible greet them when they arrive and see them out when they leave)*

5. **Do your job with confidence.** *(Research when necessary but don't doubt yourself in front of students, their families, or your employees)*

6. **Practice the "Golden Rule"** *(Be honest, have good manners, be genuinely interested in students and families, demonstrate integrity and know your boundaries with customers, vendors, neighbors, acquaintances)*

7. **Leave personal baggage at home.** *(Don't take personal issues to work)*

8. **Take your responsibilities seriously but not yourself.**

9. **Remember, the customer is always right, even when their wrong.**

10. **Don't be afraid or feel guilty about asking for payment.** *(You provide a service and customers expect to pay you for it)*

11. **Encourage and reward referrals – Word of Mouth (WOM) is your greatest ally, if you are good at your job. Your current customers all have family, friends, and neighbors that can benefit from what you offer.** *(Encourage guest attendance, give discounts, free classes, etc)*

12. **Pay your business bills on time.** *(Word travels fast, be responsible)*

13. **"Sales" is <u>Not</u> a dirty word.** *(It is a technique for removing obstacles)*

14. **Be an expert in your field, but don't try to be an expert in every field.** *(Hire or trade with people for the jobs you do not know, e.g. bookkeeper, electrician, plumber, etc.)*

15. **Do not delegate the money.** *(Account for the money personally)*

16. **Set yourself up for success.** *(Negotiating your lease, business software, automated billing, re-model occasionally, schedule activities, etc.)*

17. **Find good, dependable, fair-priced vendors and be loyal to them so long as they treat you well.** *(Not necessarily the cheapest – you will be dealing with them for years - quality products & flexible options with first name basis people where a mutual trust exists are more important)*

18. **Buy what you can from businesses in your neighborhood** *(Their well-being is tied to yours; copies/printing, office supplies, lunch, etc.)*

19. **Leave it at the office.** *(Go home at night with peace of mind. It's OK to think about your work when you are home, but only by choice)*

20. **LOOK FORWARD TO YOUR JOB!**
(If you don't look forward to your chosen career, find another)

BIBLIOGRAPHY

Deadman, Peter. <u>A Manual of Acupuncture</u>. 1998 Journal of Medcine Publications, 22 Cromwell Rd Hove East Sussex BN3 3EB England

Parker, Edmund K. <u>Infinite Insights into Kenpo Series 1-5</u>. 1982 Delsby Publications, Pasadena California

Parker, Edmund K. <u>Encyclopedia of Kenpo</u>. 1992 Delsby Publications, Pasadena California

Liu, Sing-Han. Ba Gua: Hidden Knowledge in the Taoist Internal Martial Art. 1998 Liu Sing-Han and Bracy, John Publishing

Adams, Brian. The Medical Implications of Karate Blows. Published 1969

Howstuffworks.com
Nutritiondata.com
Webmd.com
Mathisfun.com
Molossia.org
Wingchunonline.com
Scientificpsychic.com
Nlh.nih.gov/medlineplus
Pitt.edu
Mediral.com
Your-doctor.com
Scribd.com

ABOUT THE AUTHOR

Barry Barker (aka Mr. B), is the father of 5 kids, has 6 grandkids, and 78 Black Belts as of this 2018 update (See Black Belt Family Tree below). He is a 9th Degree Black Belt in this Kenpo system, a Licensed Acupuncturist, full-time school owner, and teacher for over 30 years, running Poway Kenpo Karate/Poway Martial Arts, which he founded in 1984.

Mr. Barker became interested in martial arts after watching Bruce Lee as a child. He first enrolled in martial arts at Brian Adams Kenpo Karate School in San Diego, California in 1973, with Parker Linekin as his instructor.

Mr. Barker then dabbled in various martial arts styles until he found an Ed Parker Kenpo Karate School in 1980, located in El Cajon, California. That school was run by a very technical instructor and private student of Mr. Parker, Jim Mitchell (does the stance work photos in Mr. Parker's Book #2). Mr. Barker earned his 1st Degree Black Belt at this school in 1983, with Mr. Parker as a member of his testing board.

In 1984, Jim Mitchell promoted Mr. Barker to 2nd Degree Black Belt and in the same year he opened Aaction Kenpo Karate, as a Jim Mitchell affiliate school, later changed to Poway Kenpo Karate.

He was promoted to 3rd Degree in 1987 and 4th Degree in 1990. Mr. Mitchell moved out of state shortly after so Mr. Barker formed his own Kenpo Association, the American Kenpo Alliance (AKA) in 1992, to administer to his own Kenpo students.

Additional certification came in 1994 by Orned "Chicken" Gabriel and Steve "Nasty" Anderson, recognizing Mr. Barker as a 4th Degree in their United Karate Federation (UKF). IKKA Master Instructor Ernest George Jr. promoted Mr. Barker to 5th Degree in 1995 then 6th Degree in 2000.

While continuing to teach Kenpo students, Mr. Barker expanded his training facility in 1998 when he opened a Muay Thai gym called World Class Kickboxing, later becoming The Boxing Club. He added Brazilian Jiu Jitsu in 2005 and MMA in 2008. All of that became part of what is now Poway Martial Arts.

He was promoted to 7th Degree in 2005 by Masters Rick Hughes and Willy Steele, both Ed Parker Black Belts and IKKA Master Instructors'. In 2010 he was promoted to 8th Degree by GM Parker Linekin, with additional authorization provided from SGM Brian Adams. In 2015 he was promoted to 9th Degree as authorized by SGM Brian Adams, GM Parker Linekin, GM Orned "Chicken" Gabriel, and GM Reynaldo Leal.

In addition to running Poway Kenpo Karate and Poway Martial Arts, Mr. Barker pursued his education and graduated from Pacific College of Oriental Medicine with a Master's Degree in Traditional Oriental Medicine (MSTOM) in 2007. He is a Nationally Certified (Dipl. O.M.) and California Licensed Acupuncturist (L.Ac.).

This Mind-Body-Spirit book series is a project he gave himself to further his personal growth and contribute to the martial arts community.

Mr. Barker continues to run Poway Kenpo Karate and Poway Martial Arts while practicing Acupuncture. In 2014, his school celebrated 30 years in business, and is highly regarded in the local community. As an avid learner and student of martial arts, Mr. Barker has also sought additional training over the years to continue and enhance his own skills.

Additional training:
Ed Parker, Advanced Kenpo Theory • Jeff Speakman, Kenpo Seminar • Joe Lewis, several Fight Training Seminars • Steve Nasty Anderson, several Fight Training Seminars • Orned Chicken Gabriel, 2 Years Personal Training & many Fight Training Seminars • Brian Adams, Knife & Stick Fighting Seminar • Dave Hebler, Power & Speed Seminar • Richard Post, Knife Fighting Seminar • Rick Hughes, many Classes & Seminars • Willy Steele, many Classes & Seminars • Toke Hill, Olympic Style Sparring Seminar • Mike Stone, Martial Arts Seminars • Eric Lee, Martial Arts Training Seminar • Parker Linekin, many years of Seminars & Training • John Denora, Daito Ryu Seminar • George Dillman, Pressure Point Seminar • Prof. Wally Jay, several Small Circle Jiu Jitsu Seminars • Royce Gracie, Brazilian Jiu Jitsu Seminars • Nelson Monteiro, Brazilian Jiu Jitsu 2 Years Training & Seminars • Carlos Valente, Brazilian Jiu Jitsu 1 Year Training and Seminars • Vic Zamora, Boxing Personal Training • Vincent Soberano, Muay Thai Personal Training • Melchor Menor, Muay Thai Seminars & Classes • Nelson Siyavong, several Muay Thai Seminars • Kaewsamrit Muay Thai Training Camp, 2 Weeks Bangkok Thailand • Cepeda Brothers, Arnis de Mano Classes • Krav Maga, Certification Seminar • CDT, Certification Seminar • Cung Lee, San Shou Seminar • Jim Tian, Tai Chi Chuan several years • Frank Primicias, Lo Han Chi Gung Seminars • Chen Sitan, Taiji Seminar • Rey Leal, Tai Chi Personal Training • International Training Program, Chengdu University of Chinese Medicine in Chengdu, China

Mr. Barker has been recognized more formally in other ways. Those recognitions are listed below:

- Inducted Golden Global Martial Arts Hall of Fame 1998
- Inducted Masters Hall of Fame 2000
- Inducted World Amateur Martial Arts International Federation 2006
- Listed Heritage Registry of Who's Who 2007
- City of Poway Mayors Commendation for Civic Work 2010 & 2014
- CA State Senate Community Service Commendation 2012, 2014, 2017
- Inducted USA Martial Arts Hall of Fame 2014
- Presidential Fitness Award 2017

2017 Black Belt Family Tree

AMERICAN KENPO ALLIANCE LINEAGE

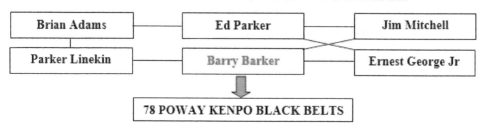

| Brian Adams | Ed Parker | Jim Mitchell |
| Parker Linekin | Barry Barker | Ernest George Jr |

78 POWAY KENPO BLACK BELTS

Tim Mullins 6th Degree	Rosie Barker 6th Degree	Bryan Taylor 6th Degree	Heath Gross 5th Degree	Dai Phipps 5th Degree
Josh Lara-Barker 5th Degree	Brian Gist 5th Degree	Jody Wall 5th Degree	Dave Arnold 4th Degree	John Hippen 4th Degree
Jordan Barker 4th Degree	Jason Gonzales 3rd Degree	John Weaver 3rd Degree	Daniel Barnier 3rd Degree	Dan Dier 3rd Degree
Dave Rosenberg 3rd Degree	Lisa Jackson 2nd Degree	Nicola Ruskin 2nd Degree	Kyle Froland 2nd Degree	Alex Stanich 2nd Degree
Denise Ellison 2nd Degree	Ryan Ellison 2nd Degree	Ian Bloom 2nd Degree	Ray Munoz 2nd Degree	Dave Dunn 2nd Degree
Cassie Li 2nd Degree	G Vanderloop 2nd Degree	Obleo Nobles 2nd Degree	Tyson Bowen 2nd Degree	Vinka Valdivia 2nd Degree
Colleen Heller 2nd Degree	Patty Alvarez 2nd Degree	Justin Slawson 2nd Degree	Eric Bressinger 2nd Degree	Gabe Bugayong 2nd Degree
Aidan Bell 2nd Degree	Sheri Hughes 1st Degree	Daniel Wolsey 1st Degree	Brian Eisenberg 1st Degree	Jim Loevenguth 1st Degree
Jon Fear 1st Degree	Ed Theodore 1st Degree	Chuck Murphy 1st Degree	Randy Evans 1st Degree	Tara Trujillo 1st Degree
Aimee Trujillo 1st Degree	Eric Aguigam 1st Degree	Brandon Reed 1st Degree	Mike Leong 1st Degree	Trevor Jackson 1st Degree
Roy Sarmiento 1st Degree	Maranda Li 1st Degree	Colby Brownlee 1st Degree	Scott Hoffman 1st Degree	Tyler Hammond 1st Degree
Steve Mattson 1st Degree	Chandler Robak 1st Degree	Joey Balistreri 1st Degree	Kyle Strommer 1st Degree	Ryan Strommer 1st Degree
Quinn Simpson 1st Degree	Bryan Bloom 1st Degree	Brian Siemienczuk 1st Degree	Aaron Harlan 1st Degree	Erin Figueroa 1st Degree
Hailey Sokoloff 1st Degree	Josh Bauserman 1st Degree	Riley Hammond 1st Degree	Zach Smith 1st Degree	Jessica Lara Davis 1st Degree
Mark Davis 1st Degree	Chris Santillo 1st Degree	Kierstin Rowell 1st Degree	Stevan White 1st Degree	Oscar Cruz 1st Degree
Kaylee Mayer 1st Degree	Savannah Mayer 1st Degree	Ethan Champion 1st Degree		

Made in the USA
Columbia, SC
25 June 2018